The Emotional Intelligence Handbook

Practical Strategies to Enhance Your Relationships, Career, and Well-Being

Alexandra Hart

CONTENTS

Introduction to "The Emotional Intelligence Handbook"

Welcome to **"The Emotional Intelligence Handbook: Practical Strategies to Enhance Your Relationships, Career, and Well-Being."** Whether you're a student, a professional, or someone who simply wants to improve their emotional well-being, this book is your guide to developing and harnessing the power of Emotional Intelligence (EI). I'm Alexandra Hart, and I'm thrilled to accompany you on this transformative journey.

Why Emotional Intelligence?

In today's fast-paced world, the ability to understand and manage our emotions, as well as the emotions of others, has become more crucial than ever. Emotional Intelligence is the key to building stronger relationships, excelling in your career, and achieving a sense of inner peace and fulfillment.

Research has shown that people with high EI are more likely to succeed in their personal and professional lives. They can navigate social complexities, lead and motivate others, and excel in their careers while also maintaining healthy relationships. EI is not just about feeling good; it's about doing well and living a balanced, harmonious life.

How to Use This Book

This book is designed to be a comprehensive, practical guide to developing your Emotional Intelligence. Each chapter focuses on a different aspect of EI and provides you with actionable strategies and exercises to enhance your skills. Here's a step-by-step process to make the most out of this book:

Step 1: Understanding the Foundations of Emotional Intelligence

Before diving into the practical exercises, it's essential to understand the core components of EI. The first few chapters will introduce you to the fundamental concepts:

1. **Self-Awareness**: Recognizing and understanding your emotions.

2. **Self-Regulation**: Managing your emotions effectively.

3. **Motivation**: Harnessing intrinsic motivation to achieve your goals.

4. **Empathy**: Understanding and sharing the feelings of others.

5. **Social Skills**: Building strong interpersonal relation-

ships.

Take your time with these chapters. Reflect on your current level of EI and identify areas where you can improve. Each concept is explained in detail, with real-life examples to help you relate to the material.

Step 2: Applying Emotional Intelligence in Different Contexts

Once you have a solid understanding of the basics, the next chapters will guide you on how to apply EI in various aspects of your life:

1. **Romantic Relationships**: Enhancing emotional connection and overcoming challenges.

2. **Family Dynamics**: Building stronger bonds and navigating conflicts.

3. **Friendships**: Deepening connections and managing misunderstandings.

4. **The Workplace**: Improving professional relationships, teamwork, and leadership.

These chapters provide specific strategies and personal stories to illustrate how EI can transform your interactions and relationships. Pay close attention to the examples and think about how you can apply these strategies in your own life.

Step 3: Practical Exercises and Activities

The heart of this book lies in the practical exercises and activities designed to enhance your EI. Here's how to approach these exercises:

1. **Daily Practices**: Incorporate daily practices like mindfulness meditation, gratitude journaling, and emotional check-ins into your routine. These practices will help you stay connected to your emotions and improve your overall emotional well-being.

   - **Mindfulness Meditation**: Set aside 10-15 minutes each day to practice mindfulness meditation. Focus on your breath and stay present, gently bringing your attention back whenever your mind wanders.

   - **Gratitude Journaling**: Each day, write down three things you are grateful for. Reflecting on positive experiences can enhance your overall emotional well-being.

   - **Emotional Check-Ins**: Regularly ask yourself, "How am I feeling right now?" and "What might be causing these feelings?" This practice helps you stay connected to your emotions and understand their impact on your behavior.

2. **Exercises for Improving Self-Awareness, Self-Regu-

lation, Empathy, and Social Skills: Follow the detailed steps provided in each exercise to develop specific EI skills. Practice regularly and track your progress.

- **Self-Awareness Exercise**: Practice body scan meditation to become more aware of your physical and emotional state.

- **Self-Regulation Exercise**: Use techniques like deep breathing and positive self-talk to manage your emotions effectively.

- **Empathy Exercise**: Engage in perspective-taking to understand others' feelings and viewpoints.

- **Social Skills Exercise**: Practice active listening and effective communication to strengthen your interpersonal relationships.

3. **Journaling Prompts and Reflection Activities**: Use the journaling prompts and reflection activities to deepen your understanding and application of EI. Reflect on your experiences and identify areas for improvement.

- **Self-Awareness Journaling Prompt**: Reflect on a recent situation where you felt a strong emotion. Describe the situation, the emotion, and how you responded.

- **Self-Regulation Journaling Prompt**: Think of a time when you successfully managed a difficult emotion. Describe the situation, the strategies you used, and what you learned.

- **Empathy Journaling Prompt**: Reflect on a recent interaction where you felt empathy for someone. Describe the situation, the person's emotions, and your response.

- **Social Skills Journaling Prompt**: Think of a recent conversation where you communicated effectively. Describe the conversation, the strategies you used, and what you learned.

Step 4: Building a Support System

Developing EI is a continuous journey, and having a support system can make a significant difference. Here's how to build and leverage your support system:

1. **Find a Mentor or Coach**: Seek out someone with high EI who can guide you on your journey. This could be a teacher, counselor, or experienced colleague. Regularly check in with your mentor, share your progress, and seek their advice.

2. **Join a Community**: Look for groups or communities focused on personal development and EI. These could be

online forums, local meetups, or professional organizations. Engaging with like-minded individuals can provide valuable insights and encouragement.

3. **Share Your Journey**: Don't be afraid to share your EI journey with friends and family. They can offer support, feedback, and accountability. Plus, sharing your experiences can inspire others to develop their EI as well.

Step 5: Reflecting on Your Progress

Regular reflection is crucial for continuous improvement. Here are some ways to reflect on your EI journey:

1. **Keep a Journal**: Maintain a journal where you document your experiences, challenges, and achievements. Reflect on your growth and identify areas for further improvement.

2. **Set Regular Check-Ins**: Schedule regular check-ins with yourself to assess your progress. Ask yourself questions like, "How have I improved in managing my emotions?" and "What areas still need work?"

3. **Celebrate Successes**: Acknowledge and celebrate your successes, no matter how small. Recognizing your progress can boost your motivation and reinforce positive behaviors.

Step 6: Staying Committed to Your Journey

Developing EI is a lifelong commitment. Here are some tips to stay committed to your journey:

1. **Set Long-Term Goals**: In addition to short-term goals, set long-term goals for your EI development. These goals can provide a sense of direction and purpose.

2. **Stay Curious**: Cultivate a mindset of lifelong learning. Stay open to new experiences and continue seeking knowledge about EI and personal growth.

3. **Practice Self-Compassion**: Be kind to yourself throughout your journey. Understand that developing EI takes time and effort, and it's okay to encounter setbacks. Practice self-compassion and keep moving forward.

Final Thoughts

"The Emotional Intelligence Handbook" is more than just a book; it's a guide to transforming your life through the power of Emotional Intelligence. By following the step-by-step process outlined in this book, you can develop the skills needed to enhance your relationships, career, and overall well-being.

Remember, the journey to developing EI is ongoing. Stay committed, embrace the process, and celebrate your progress. With dedication and practice, you can unlock the full potential of Emotional Intelligence and create a more fulfilling and successful life.

I'm excited to join you on this journey. Let's get started!

1

Understanding Emotional Intelligence

Introduction

Hey there! Let's dive into something really fascinating that can transform your life: Emotional Intelligence, or EI for short. Unlike traditional IQ, which measures how smart you are in terms of logical reasoning and problem-solving, EI is all about being smart with your emotions. It's about recognizing, understanding, and managing not just your own emotions but also those of others. Sounds powerful, right? In this chapter, we'll break down what EI is, why it's important, and how it impacts your relationships.

Components of Emotional Intelligence

So, what exactly makes up Emotional Intelligence? There are five key components: self-awareness, self-regulation, motivation, empathy, and social skills. Let's explore each one in detail.

1. **Self-awareness**

Self-awareness is the foundation of EI. It's about knowing what you're feeling and why. Imagine you had a tough day at work, and you're feeling irritable. Self-awareness is that little voice in your head saying, "Hey, I'm feeling stressed because of that meeting earlier." Understanding your emotions helps you handle them better.

Example

: Reflect on a recent situation where you felt a strong emotion. How did it impact your actions? Maybe you snapped at a friend because you were stressed. Recognizing this is the first step towards change.

2. **Self-regulation**

Now that you know what you're feeling, the next step is managing those emotions. Self-regulation is all about controlling your reactions, especially in challenging situations. It's like being the captain of your emotional ship, steering it calmly through stormy seas.

Techniques

: Deep breathing, mindfulness, and cognitive reframing can help you manage emotions. Try taking a few deep breaths next time you feel overwhelmed. It works wonders!

3. **Motivation**

Motivation in the context of EI is about having the drive to pursue goals with energy and persistence. It's what keeps you going, even when the going gets tough. Motivated people tend to be more optimistic and resilient.

Example

: Set clear, achievable goals and celebrate small victories along the way. This can boost your motivation and keep you on track.

4. **Empathy**

Empathy is the ability to understand and share the feelings of others. It's about putting yourself in someone else's shoes and feeling what they feel. Empathy builds deeper, more meaningful connections.

Practice

: Engage in active listening. When someone is talking, really focus on what they're saying without interrupting. Try to understand their perspective fully.

5. **Social Skills**

Finally, social skills are about interacting well with others. It's about effective communication, collaboration, and conflict resolution. Good social skills can enhance both personal and professional relationships.

Example

: Practice clear and open communication. When discussing a problem, focus on the issue, not the person. This helps in resolving conflicts amicably.

The Science Behind Emotional Intelligence

You might be wondering, "Is there any science behind this?" Absolutely! Research shows that EI has a neurological basis. Our brain's limbic system, which regulates emotions, and the prefrontal cortex, which handles decision-making, work together to shape our emotional responses. Studies have found that people with high EI tend to have better mental health, job performance, and leadership skills.

Scientific Insights: Neuroimaging studies have shown that individuals with high EI have greater activity in the prefrontal cortex, which is responsible for executive functions like decision-making, and in the amygdala, which processes emotions. This increased activity allows for better regulation of emotions and more thoughtful responses to emotional stimuli.

Research Findings: A study by Dr. Daniel Goleman, a pioneer in the field of EI, found that emotional intelligence is twice as important as technical skills and IQ in determining outstanding job performance. People with high EI are more adaptable, resilient, and able to navigate complex social environments effectively.

Impact of Emotional Intelligence on Relationships

Now, let's talk about why EI is a game-changer for relationships.

- **Self-awareness**: When you're aware of your own emotions, you understand your needs and desires better. This clarity helps in communicating effectively with your partner or friends.

  Example: If you're feeling upset, instead of lashing out, you can express your feelings calmly, saying something like, "I'm feeling really stressed right now because of work, and I need some time to unwind."

- **Self-regulation**: By managing your emotions, you can avoid unnecessary conflicts and handle disagreements calmly. It's like bringing a sense of peace into your relationships.
  Example: If you're angry during a disagreement, taking a moment to breathe and collect your thoughts can prevent the situation from escalating.

- **Empathy**: Understanding others' emotions leads to deeper connections and trust. When you show empathy, people feel valued and understood.
  Example: If a friend is going through a tough time, showing empathy by listening and offering support can strengthen your bond.

- **Social Skills**: Good social skills enhance your interactions, making them more positive and productive. Whether it's collaborating on a project or resolving a dispute, social skills make a huge difference.
  Example: Practicing active listening and being open to feedback during team meetings can improve collaboration and lead to better outcomes.

Practical Tips and Exercises

Here are some easy-to-follow exercises to boost your EI:

1. **Self-awareness Exercise**: Keep a daily journal of your emotions. Write down what you felt and why. Reflect on any patterns you notice.

   Detailed Practice: Set aside 10 minutes each evening to write in your journal. Start by noting the strongest emotions you felt during the day. Describe the situation that triggered these emotions and how you responded. Over time, look for patterns. Do certain situations consistently trigger the same emotions? How do your responses affect the outcomes?

2. **Self-regulation Technique**: Practice mindfulness meditation for 10 minutes each day. Focus on your breath and let go of any distracting thoughts.

   Detailed Practice: Find a quiet space and sit comfortably. Close your eyes and take deep breaths, focusing on the sensation of air entering and leaving your body. If your mind wanders, gently bring your focus back to your breath. This practice can help you stay calm and centered, even in stressful situations.

3. **Empathy Practice**: Next time you're in a conversation, listen without planning your response. Just focus on understanding the other person's point of view.

   Detailed Practice: During your next conversation, make

a conscious effort to listen more than you speak. Pay attention to the speaker's words, tone, and body language. Ask open-ended questions to encourage them to share more. Reflect back what you've heard to show that you're engaged and understanding their perspective.

4. **Motivation Exercise**: Set a personal goal and break it down into smaller, manageable tasks. Celebrate each small achievement to stay motivated.

   Detailed Practice: Identify a goal, such as learning a new skill. Break it down into daily or weekly tasks. For example, if you want to learn to play the guitar, set a goal to practice for 20 minutes each day. Celebrate your progress by treating yourself to something small, like watching an episode of your favorite show after a successful practice session.

5. **Social Skills Practice**: Work on improving your communication skills by engaging in active listening and being mindful of non-verbal cues.

   Detailed Practice: During conversations, make eye contact, nod to show you're listening, and use open body language. Avoid interrupting the speaker. When it's your turn to speak, summarize what you've heard to ensure understanding before sharing your thoughts.

Conclusion

Emotional Intelligence is more than just a buzzword; it's a powerful skill that can enhance every aspect of your life, especially your relationships. By understanding and applying the components of EI—self-awareness, self-regulation, motivation, empathy, and social skills—you can create more fulfilling and harmonious connections with others. In the next chapter, we'll dive deeper into self-awareness and explore practical ways to improve this essential skill.

2

Self-Awareness

Introduction

In the last chapter, we touched on the basics of Emotional Intelligence (EI) and its components. Now, let's take a deeper dive into the first and arguably most crucial component: self-awareness. Self-awareness is like having a built-in GPS for your emotions, guiding you through life's ups and downs with clarity and insight. In this chapter, we'll explore what self-awareness is, why it's important, and how you can cultivate it to enhance your life and relationships.

Understanding Self-Awareness

Self-awareness means being conscious of your own thoughts, feelings, and behaviors. It's about knowing your strengths and weaknesses, understanding what triggers your emotions, and recognizing how your actions affect others. There are two types of self-awareness: internal and external. Internal self-awareness involves being aware of your inner world—your thoughts, feelings, values, and beliefs. External self-awareness is about understanding how others perceive you and recognizing the impact of your actions and behavior on those around you.

Imagine you're feeling anxious about an upcoming exam. Internal self-awareness helps you recognize that this anxiety stems from a fear of failure. External self-awareness might reveal that your nervous energy is affecting your friends, who are trying to study with you. Being self-aware offers numerous benefits, including improved decision-making, enhanced emotional regulation, and better relationships. When you understand your emotions, you can make more informed choices, manage your reactions better, and have more honest and meaningful interactions with others.

Take Jane, a high school teacher. Jane noticed she often felt overwhelmed during parent-teacher meetings. Through self-awareness practices like journaling, she realized this was because she felt unprepared. By addressing this issue, she started preparing notes ahead of meetings, reducing her stress and improving her interactions with parents. Similarly, Alex, a software engineer, struggled with time management. He often felt overwhelmed by deadlines. By keeping a journal, he realized he was procrastinating because he felt intimidated by large tasks. Breaking tasks into smaller, manageable steps helped him improve his productivity.

Developing self-awareness takes practice. Writing down your thoughts and feelings can help you identify patterns and triggers. Set aside 10 minutes each evening to write in your journal. Start by noting the strongest emotions you felt during the day. Describe the situation that triggered these emotions and how you responded. Over time, look for patterns. Do certain situations consistently trigger the same emotions? How do your responses affect the outcomes? Engaging in regular mindfulness meditation helps you stay present and aware of your emotions. Find a quiet space and sit comfortably. Close your eyes and take deep breaths, focusing on the sensation of air entering and leaving your body. If your mind wanders, gently bring your focus back to your breath. This practice can help you stay calm and centered, even in stressful situations.

Asking friends and colleagues for constructive feedback can provide insights into how others perceive you. Approach a trusted friend or colleague and ask for their honest feedback about your behavior and how you come across in different situations. Be open to their observations and reflect on how this feedback aligns with your self-perception. For example, Maria, a college student, felt isolated because she thought her friends didn't like her. Through mindfulness practices, she recognized her negative self-talk and replaced it with positive affirmations. This shift in mindset helped her feel more confident and connected with her friends.

Self-awareness isn't just a feel-good concept; it has a solid scientific foundation. Research shows that self-awareness is linked to various positive outcomes, including better academic performance, enhanced creativity, and improved mental health. A study published in the journal *Emotion* found that individuals with high self-awareness are more likely to have better emotional regulation skills. This means they can handle stress and anxiety more effectively than those with low self-awareness. According to research from the Harvard Business Review, self-aware leaders are more effective. Teams led by self-aware individuals tend to have higher job satisfaction and better overall performance. Data from a 2018 study by Tasha Eurich, an organizational psychologist, revealed that while 95% of people think they are self-aware, only about 10-15% actually are. This gap highlights the importance of actively working on self-awareness.

Here are some easy-to-follow exercises to boost your self-aware-ness:

1. **Daily Reflection**: At the end of each day, reflect on three things that went well and three things that didn't. Consider your emotional responses to these events. Write down three positive experiences and three challenges you faced. Reflect on your emotional responses and what you learned from these situations. For example, if you felt proud after completing a project, note what aspects of the task made you feel this way. If you felt frustrated during a conversation, consider why you felt that way and how you might handle it differently next time.

2. **Emotional Check-In**: Set a timer to go off three times a day. When it does, take a moment to check in with your emotions. What are you feeling? Why do you think you're feeling that way? When the timer goes off, pause whatever you're doing and take a few deep breaths. Ask yourself, "What am I feeling right now?" and "Why am I feeling this way?" Note your responses in a journal. Over time,

you'll start to see patterns and gain deeper insights into your emotional landscape.

3. **Feedback Loop**: Regularly seek feedback from a trusted friend or mentor. Discuss specific situations where you'd like their perspective. Choose a specific situation, like a presentation or a meeting, and ask for feedback on your performance. Use this feedback to identify areas for improvement and celebrate your strengths. For example, if a colleague mentions that you tend to dominate conversations in meetings, work on listening more and encouraging others to share their ideas.

4. **Mindfulness Meditation**: Engage in regular mindfulness meditation to enhance your awareness of the present moment. Dedicate 10-15 minutes each day to mindfulness meditation. Sit comfortably, close your eyes, and focus on your breath. If your mind starts to wander, gently bring your attention back to your breath. This practice helps you stay present and aware of your thoughts and feelings without getting overwhelmed by them.

5. **Values Clarification**: Understanding your core values can enhance self-awareness. Spend some time identifying your values and consider how they influence your decisions and behaviors. For example, if you value honesty, reflect on how this value shapes your interactions with others. Make a list of your top five values and write about

how they impact your daily life.

6. **Strengths and Weaknesses Assessment**: Take time to assess your strengths and weaknesses. Knowing what you're good at and where you need improvement can provide a clearer picture of yourself. Write down your strengths and how you can leverage them in your life. Similarly, list your weaknesses and think about strategies to improve in these areas.

To see how self-awareness can make a difference, let's explore some real-life scenarios. Imagine you're in a heated argument with a friend. Without self-awareness, you might say things you later regret. But with self-awareness, you recognize your rising anger and choose to take a few deep breaths before responding. This pause allows you to respond more calmly and constructively, preserving the relationship. At work, you're feeling unappreciated and overworked. Self-awareness helps you identify these feelings and understand that they're affecting your motivation. By acknowledging these emotions, you can have a productive conversation with your manager about your workload and seek solutions. You're preparing for a big exam, but you're feeling anxious and distracted. Self-awareness helps you realize that your anxiety is coming from a fear of failure. By recognizing this, you can implement strategies to manage your anxiety, such as breaking your study sessions into smaller chunks and taking regular breaks.

Building self-awareness is an ongoing process. It's not something you achieve overnight, but with consistent practice, you can enhance this crucial skill. Start small, begin with simple exercises like daily reflection or emotional check-ins. Gradually incorporate more practices like journaling and seeking feedback. Be patient, developing self-awareness takes time. Be patient with yourself and recognize that progress may be slow but steady. Stay committed, make self-awareness a regular part of your routine. The more you practice, the more natural it will become.

Self-awareness is a powerful tool that can significantly enhance your life. By understanding your emotions and behaviors, you can make better decisions, manage your reactions, and build stronger relationships. In the next chapter, we'll explore self-regulation and how you can develop the skills to manage your emotions effectively.

3

SELF-REGULATION

Introduction

Hey there! In the last chapter, we explored the importance of self-awareness and how it can help you understand your emotions and behaviors. Now, let's dive into the next crucial component of Emotional Intelligence (EI): self-regulation. Self-regulation is all about managing your emotions effectively. It's like being the driver of your emotional car, steering it in the right direction even when the road gets bumpy. In this chapter, we'll explore what self-regulation is, why it's important, and how you can develop this skill to enhance your life and relationships.

Understanding Self-Regulation

Self-regulation is the ability to control your emotions, thoughts, and behaviors in different situations. It's about staying calm under pressure, resisting impulsive actions, and thinking before you act. Essentially, self-regulation allows you to respond to situations in a way that aligns with your long-term goals and values rather than reacting impulsively.

Imagine you're stuck in traffic and running late for an important meeting. Without self-regulation, you might honk your horn, yell, or feel overwhelmingly frustrated. With self-regulation, you recognize your frustration, take a deep breath, and remind yourself that getting upset won't help you arrive any faster. Instead, you use the time to listen to a podcast or plan your meeting notes.

Benefits of Self-Regulation

Self-regulation offers numerous benefits, including:

- **Improved Decision-Making**: When you can manage your emotions, you make more rational and thoughtful decisions.

- **Better Relationships**: By controlling your reactions, you can handle conflicts more effectively and maintain healthier relationships.

- **Increased Productivity**: Staying focused and avoiding distractions helps you achieve your goals more efficiently.

Personal Example: Consider John, a college student who often felt overwhelmed during exams. By practicing self-regulation techniques like deep breathing and positive self-talk, he managed to stay calm during tests. This not only improved his performance but also reduced his overall stress levels.

Let's delve deeper into John's journey as a college student who learned to manage his exam stress through self-regulation techniques. This step-by-step process will highlight how he practiced self-regulation to improve his performance and reduce his overall stress levels.

Step 1: Recognizing the Problem

John often felt overwhelmed during exams. He noticed that his heart would race, his palms would sweat, and his mind would go blank as soon as he sat down to take a test. These physical and emotional reactions made it difficult for him to concentrate and perform well.

- **Self-Awareness**: The first step for John was recognizing and acknowledging his problem. He realized that his stress and anxiety were hindering his exam performance and affecting his overall well-being.

Step 2: Seeking Solutions

John knew he needed to find ways to manage his stress and improve his exam performance. He began by researching various self-regulation techniques that could help him stay calm and focused.

- **Research**: John explored articles, books, and online resources about stress management and self-regulation. He discovered several techniques that seemed promising, including deep breathing exercises and positive self-talk.

Step 3: Practicing Deep Breathing

One of the techniques John decided to try was deep breathing.

Deep breathing helps calm the nervous system, reduce stress, and improve focus.

- **Detailed Practice**: John set aside a few minutes each day to practice deep breathing. He found a quiet place to sit comfortably and closed his eyes. He inhaled deeply through his nose, filling his lungs with air, held his breath for a few seconds, and then exhaled slowly through his mouth. He repeated this process several times until he felt more relaxed.

- **Implementation During Exams**: On exam days, John used deep breathing exercises to calm his nerves before the test started. Whenever he felt anxious during the exam, he took a few deep breaths to regain his focus.

Step 4: Using Positive Self-Talk

Another technique John found helpful was positive self-talk. This involves replacing negative thoughts with positive and encouraging ones.

- **Detailed Practice**: John wrote down a list of positive affirmations and encouraging statements. Some of his favorites were, "I am well-prepared and capable," "I can handle this challenge," and "I am calm and focused."

- **Implementation During Exams**: Before the exam, John spent a few minutes repeating these affirmations to himself. Whenever he felt anxious during the test, he reminded himself of these positive statements to boost his confidence and stay focused.

Step 5: Creating a Study Routine

John realized that part of his stress came from feeling unprepared. He decided to create a structured study routine to ensure he was well-prepared for his exams.

- **Detailed Practice**: John set specific study times each day and created a study schedule that covered all the material he needed to review. He included regular breaks to avoid burnout and used techniques like active recall and spaced repetition to enhance his learning.

- **Implementation**: By following his study routine consistently, John felt more confident in his knowledge and better prepared for his exams. This preparation reduced his anxiety and made it easier for him to stay calm during tests.

Step 6: Reflecting on Progress

John regularly reflected on his progress and adjusted his strategies as needed. He kept a journal where he recorded his experiences, what worked well, and what could be improved.

- **Detailed Practice**: After each exam, John wrote about how he felt, how well he managed his stress, and how effective his self-regulation techniques were. This reflection helped him identify areas for improvement and reinforce what worked well.

Through this step-by-step process, John successfully managed his exam stress and improved his performance. By recognizing his problem, seeking solutions, practicing deep breathing and positive self-talk, creating a study routine, and reflecting on his progress, John developed effective self-regulation skills. These skills not only helped him during exams but also contributed to his overall well-being and academic success.

By following similar steps, you too can develop self-regulation skills to manage stress and enhance your performance in various aspects of life. Remember, the journey to self-regulation and emotional intelligence is ongoing, so be patient with yourself and celebrate your progress along the way.

Techniques to Develop Self-Regulation

Developing self-regulation takes practice and patience. Here are some techniques to help you get started:

1. **Mindfulness Meditation**: Regular mindfulness practice can help you stay present and manage your emotions better.

   - **Detailed Practice**: Dedicate 10-15 minutes each day to mindfulness meditation. Sit comfortably, close your eyes, and focus on your breath. When your mind starts to wander, gently bring your attention back to your breath. This practice helps you stay calm and centered, even in stressful situations.

2. **Cognitive Reframing**: Change your perspective on challenging situations to manage your emotional responses better.

   ○ **Detailed Practice**: When faced with a difficult situation, try to view it from a different perspective. For example, if you receive negative feedback, instead of feeling discouraged, view it as an opportunity to improve and grow. Write down the situation and your initial reaction, then reframe it in a more positive light.

3. **Deep Breathing Exercises**: Deep breathing can help calm your mind and reduce stress.

   ○ **Detailed Practice**: Practice deep breathing by inhaling slowly through your nose for a count of four, holding your breath for a count of four, and exhaling slowly through your mouth for a count of four. Repeat this cycle several times until you feel more relaxed.

4. **Setting Goals**: Clear, achievable goals can help you stay focused and motivated.

   ○ **Detailed Practice**: Set specific, measurable, achievable, relevant, and time-bound (SMART) goals. Break larger goals into smaller, manageable tasks. For example, if your goal is to improve your grades, break it down into tasks like setting study times, attending review sessions, and seeking help from teachers.

5. **Self-Monitoring**: Keep track of your emotions and reactions to identify patterns and areas for improvement.

- **Detailed Practice**: Keep a journal where you record your emotions and reactions throughout the day. Note what triggered these emotions and how you responded. Over time, look for patterns and identify areas where you can improve your self-regulation.

Personal Stories and Examples

Personal stories can make the concept of self-regulation more relatable. Let's look at some examples:

Emily, a high school athlete, often felt nervous before competitions. By practicing deep breathing and visualization techniques, she managed to calm her nerves and perform better during games. David, a project manager, used to get easily frustrated with his team. He started practicing mindfulness and cognitive reframing, which helped him approach conflicts more calmly and find constructive solutions.

The Science Behind Self-Regulation

Self-regulation isn't just a useful skill; it has a strong scientific basis. Research shows that self-regulation is linked to various positive outcomes, including better academic performance, enhanced emotional well-being, and improved interpersonal relationships.

Studies and Data:

- **Self-Regulation and Academic Performance**: A study published in the journal *Psychological Science* found that self-regulation skills are predictive of academic success. Students who could delay gratification and manage their impulses tended to perform better academically (Mischel et al., 2011).

- **Self-Regulation and Stress Management**: Research from the American Psychological Association highlights the importance of self-regulation in managing stress and preventing burnout. Individuals who practice self-regulation techniques are better equipped to handle stress and maintain a positive outlook (Gross, J.J., & John, O.P., 2003).

- **Self-Regulation as a Strength**: Roy Baumeister, a leading psychologist in self-regulation research, has shown that self-regulation operates like a muscle. With regular practice, it gets stronger, improving one's ability to manage emotions and behaviors over time (Baumeister, R.F., Vohs, K.D., & Tice, D.M., 2007).

Practical Exercises

Here are some practical exercises to help you develop self-regulation:

1. **Mindfulness Meditation**: Dedicate 10-15 minutes each day to mindfulness meditation. Sit comfortably, close your eyes, and focus on your breath. When your mind starts to wander, gently bring your attention back to your breath. This practice helps you stay calm and centered, even in stressful situations.

2. **Cognitive Reframing**: When faced with a difficult situation, try to view it from a different perspective. For example, if you receive negative feedback, instead of feeling discouraged, view it as an opportunity to improve and grow. Write down the situation and your initial reaction, then reframe it in a more positive light.

3. **Deep Breathing Exercises**: Practice deep breathing by inhaling slowly through your nose for a count of four, holding your breath for a count of four, and exhaling slowly through your mouth for a count of four. Repeat this cycle several times until you feel more relaxed.

4. **Setting Goals**: Set specific, measurable, achievable, relevant, and time-bound (SMART) goals. Break larger goals into smaller, manageable tasks. For example, if your goal is to improve your grades, break it down into tasks like setting study times, attending review sessions, and seeking help from teachers.

5. **Self-Monitoring**: Keep a journal where you record your

emotions and reactions throughout the day. Note what triggered these emotions and how you responded. Over time, look for patterns and identify areas where you can improve your self-regulation.

6. **Progressive Muscle Relaxation**: This technique helps reduce physical tension and promotes relaxation. Starting from your toes, tense each muscle group for a few seconds, then slowly release the tension. Move up through your body, finishing with your head and neck.

7. **Visualization**: Visualize yourself handling challenging situations with calmness and confidence. Imagine the details of the scenario and how you will manage your emotions effectively. This practice can prepare you mentally and emotionally for real-life challenges.

To see how self-regulation can make a difference, let's explore some real-life scenarios. Imagine you're in a heated argument with a friend. Without self-regulation, you might say things you later regret. But with self-regulation, you recognize your rising anger and choose to take a few deep breaths before responding. This pause allows you to respond more calmly and constructively, preserving the relationship. At work, you're feeling unappreciated and overworked. Self-regulation helps you identify these feelings and understand that they're affecting your motivation. By acknowledging these emotions, you can have a productive conversation with your manager about your workload and seek solutions.

You're preparing for a big exam, but you're feeling anxious and distracted. Self-regulation helps you realize that your anxiety is coming from a fear of failure. By recognizing this, you can implement strategies to manage your anxiety, such as breaking your study sessions into smaller chunks and taking regular breaks.

Building self-regulation is an ongoing process. It's not something you achieve overnight, but with consistent practice, you can enhance this crucial skill. Start small, begin with simple exercises like deep breathing or mindfulness meditation. Gradually incorporate more practices like cognitive reframing and goal setting. Be patient, developing self-regulation takes time. Be patient with yourself and recognize that progress may be slow but steady. Stay committed, make self-regulation a regular part of your routine. The more you practice, the more natural it will become.

Self-regulation is a powerful tool that can significantly enhance your life. By managing your emotions and behaviors, you can make better decisions, handle stress more effectively, and build stronger relationships. In the next chapter, we'll explore motivation and how you can harness this energy to achieve your goals and lead a fulfilling life.

4

MOTIVATION

Introduction

Hey there! In the previous chapters, we explored self-awareness and self-regulation, two crucial components of Emotional Intelligence (EI). Now, let's dive into the third key component: motivation. Motivation is the driving force that propels you to achieve your goals and overcome obstacles. It's what keeps you going, even when the going gets tough. In this chapter, we'll explore what motivation is, why it's important, and how you can harness this energy to achieve your goals and lead a fulfilling life.

Understanding Motivation

Motivation is the internal process that initiates, guides, and sustains goal-oriented behaviors. It's what causes you to take action, whether it's studying for an exam, going to the gym, or pursuing a long-term career goal. There are two main types of motivation: intrinsic and extrinsic.

1. **Intrinsic Motivation**: This comes from within. It's when you do something because you find it personally rewarding. For example, you might study hard because you love learning and want to gain knowledge.

2. **Extrinsic Motivation**: This comes from external factors. It's when you do something to earn a reward or avoid punishment. For example, you might study hard to get good grades and make your parents proud.

Both types of motivation are important and can drive you to achieve your goals. However, intrinsic motivation is often more sustainable and fulfilling in the long run.

Benefits of Motivation

Motivation offers numerous benefits, including:

- **Increased Productivity**: When you're motivated, you're more focused and efficient, which leads to higher productivity.

- **Enhanced Performance**: Motivated individuals tend to perform better in both academic and professional settings.

- **Improved Well-Being**: Pursuing meaningful goals can enhance your overall sense of well-being and life satisfaction.

Personal Example: Consider Emma, a college student who loves painting. Her intrinsic motivation to create art drives her to spend hours perfecting her craft. This passion not only improves her skills but also brings her immense joy and fulfillment.

Let's explore Emma's journey as a college student who harnesses her intrinsic motivation to excel in painting. This step-by-step process will illustrate how her passion for art drives her to improve her skills and find joy and fulfillment in her craft.

Step 1: Discovering Her Passion

Emma always had an interest in art, but it wasn't until college that she discovered her true passion for painting. She found immense joy and satisfaction in expressing herself through colors and brushstrokes.

- **Self-Awareness**: The first step for Emma was recognizing her love for painting. She paid attention to how she felt while creating art and realized that painting made her feel alive and fulfilled.

Step 2: Setting Personal Goals

Emma decided to set personal goals to improve her painting skills. These goals were not about external rewards but about her desire to grow as an artist and create beautiful artwork.

- **Goal Setting**: Emma set specific, measurable, achievable, relevant, and time-bound (SMART) goals. For example, she aimed to complete one painting each week, experiment with new techniques, and attend an art workshop every semester.

Step 3: Creating a Dedicated Space and Time

To nurture her intrinsic motivation, Emma created a dedicated space and time for her painting. This environment allowed her to focus solely on her art without distractions.

- **Detailed Practice**: Emma set up a small studio in her apartment with all her painting supplies. She designated specific hours each day for painting, treating it as an important appointment she couldn't miss. This routine helped her stay consistent and disciplined.

Step 4: Embracing the Process

Emma learned to embrace the process of painting, including the challenges and setbacks. She understood that every brushstroke, even the mistakes, was part of her growth as an artist.

- **Detailed Practice**: Instead of striving for perfection, Emma focused on enjoying the creative process. She allowed herself to experiment, make mistakes, and learn from them. This mindset helped her stay motivated and resilient.

Step 5: Seeking Inspiration and Learning

To fuel her passion, Emma continuously sought inspiration and learning opportunities. She explored different art styles, studied the works of famous painters, and took art classes to enhance her skills.

- **Detailed Practice**: Emma visited art galleries, read books on painting techniques, and watched online tutorials. She also joined a local art club where she could interact with fellow artists, share ideas, and gain feedback on her work.

Step 6: Celebrating Achievements

Emma made it a point to celebrate her achievements, no matter how small. Recognizing her progress and accomplishments kept her motivated and encouraged her to keep pushing her boundaries.

- **Detailed Practice**: After completing a painting, Emma would take a moment to admire her work and reflect on what she had learned. She kept a portfolio of her paintings to track her progress over time. She also shared her artwork with friends and family, who provided positive reinforcement and support.

Step 7: Reflecting on Personal Growth

Emma regularly reflected on her personal growth as an artist. This reflection helped her stay connected to her intrinsic motivation and recognize the deeper meaning behind her passion for painting.

- **Detailed Practice**: Emma kept a journal where she wrote about her painting experiences, challenges, and breakthroughs. She reflected on how painting made her feel and how it contributed to her overall well-being and happiness. This practice deepened her connection to her art and reinforced her intrinsic motivation.

Through this step-by-step process, Emma successfully nurtured her intrinsic motivation and excelled in painting. By discovering her passion, setting personal goals, creating a dedicated space and time, embracing the process, seeking inspiration and learning, celebrating achievements, and reflecting on personal growth, Emma found immense joy and fulfillment in her art.

Her journey illustrates the power of intrinsic motivation and how it can drive you to excel in your passions. By following similar steps, you too can harness your intrinsic motivation to pursue your interests, improve your skills, and find joy and fulfillment in what you love to do. Remember, the journey is ongoing, so stay curious, embrace the process, and celebrate your progress along the way.

Techniques to Enhance Motivation

Developing and maintaining motivation takes practice and intentional effort. Here are some techniques to help you get started:

1. **Set Clear Goals**: Having specific, measurable, achievable, relevant, and time-bound (SMART) goals gives you a clear direction and purpose.

   - **Detailed Practice**: Write down your goals and break them into smaller, manageable tasks. For example, if your goal is to get fit, start with setting a target to exercise for 30 minutes three times a week.

2. **Find Your Why**: Understanding the deeper reasons behind your goals can boost your motivation.

   - **Detailed Practice**: Reflect on why your goals are important to you. Write down your reasons and revisit them whenever you feel your motivation waning.

3. **Create a Vision Board**: Visualizing your goals can make them feel more real and achievable.

   ○ **Detailed Practice**: Gather images and words that represent your goals and create a vision board. Place it somewhere you'll see it daily to remind yourself of what you're working towards.

4. **Reward Yourself**: Celebrating small victories can keep you motivated and reinforce positive behavior.

   ○ **Detailed Practice**: Set up a reward system for yourself. For example, treat yourself to something you enjoy after completing a task or reaching a milestone.

5. **Stay Positive**: Maintaining a positive mindset can help you stay motivated, even when facing challenges.

   ○ **Detailed Practice**: Practice positive self-talk and surround yourself with supportive people who encourage you to pursue your goals.

6. **Stay Accountable**: Sharing your goals with others can increase your commitment and motivation.

   ○ **Detailed Practice**: Find an accountability partner or join a group of like-minded individuals who can support and motivate you.

Personal Stories and Examples

Personal stories can make the concept of motivation more relatable. Let's look at some detailed examples:

Alex's Journey: Overcoming Academic Struggles with Vision and Goals

Alex, a high school student, had always found it difficult to stay motivated to study for exams. The pressure from his parents and teachers only added to his stress, and he often felt overwhelmed and discouraged. He spent hours staring at his textbooks, unable to concentrate, and his grades began to slip.

One day, after a particularly disheartening parent-teacher conference, Alex decided that something needed to change. He wanted to do well in school, not just to meet others' expectations but also to prove to himself that he could succeed. He realized that he needed a clearer vision of what he wanted to achieve and a plan to get there.

Alex started by setting specific goals for each of his subjects. Instead of aiming to "study more," he set a target to complete a certain number of practice problems or chapters each week. He also decided to create a vision board. He gathered images of successful students, quotes about perseverance, and pictures representing his dream college. He placed this board above his study desk where he could see it every day.

Whenever Alex felt his motivation wane, he would look at his vision board and remind himself why he was working so hard. He imagined the sense of accomplishment he would feel when he achieved his goals. Slowly but surely, Alex found that his new approach was paying off. His focus improved, he started to understand the material better, and his grades began to rise. The vision board and his clear goals gave him a tangible reminder of what he was working towards, keeping his motivation strong even during challenging times.

Maria's Fitness Journey: Finding Motivation through Community and Rewards

Maria, a recent college graduate, had always struggled with sticking to her fitness routine. She would start strong with new workout plans, only to lose interest and give up after a few weeks. She wanted to be healthier and more active, but the motivation just wasn't there.

After graduation, Maria realized that she needed to make a change for the sake of her health and well-being. She decided to find a workout buddy to keep her accountable. She reached out to her friend Lisa, who was also looking to get fit. They agreed to exercise together three times a week and set specific fitness goals, like running a certain distance or completing a workout challenge.

To keep things interesting, Maria and Lisa decided to set up a reward system. After every month of consistent workouts, they would treat themselves to a fun activity, like a spa day or a new piece of workout gear. These small rewards gave Maria something to look forward to and made the process of getting fit more enjoyable.

Having a workout buddy made a huge difference for Maria. On days when she felt like skipping a workout, Lisa's encouragement pushed her to keep going. The reward system also added an element of excitement and kept her motivated to stick with her routine. Over time, Maria noticed significant improvements in her fitness levels and overall energy. The combination of accountability and rewards helped her stay motivated and achieve her fitness goals.

The Science Behind Motivation

Motivation isn't just about willpower; it has a strong scientific foundation. Research shows that motivation is influenced by various psychological and neurological factors.

Studies and Data:

- **Self-Determination Theory**: According to this theory, proposed by Deci and Ryan, people are most motivated when they feel autonomous, competent, and connected to others. For instance, Sarah, a college student, felt more motivated to study when she had control over her schedule, felt confident in her abilities, and had supportive friends (Deci, E.L., & Ryan, R.M., 2000).

- **The Role of Dopamine**: Neuroscience research has shown that dopamine, a neurotransmitter in the brain, plays a crucial role in motivation. When you achieve a goal or anticipate a reward, your brain releases dopamine, which creates feelings of pleasure and reinforces the behavior. For example, Jake, who loves video games, feels a surge of motivation and pleasure when he completes a challenging level, thanks to dopamine (Schultz, W., 2015).

- **Goal-Setting Theory**: Proposed by Locke and Latham, this theory suggests that specific and challenging goals lead to higher performance. The act of setting goals can increase motivation and commitment. Think about how Emma, a college student, sets specific targets for her art projects and notices a boost in her motivation and productivity (Locke, E.A., & Latham, G.P., 2002).

Practical Exercises

Here are some practical exercises to help you enhance your motivation:

1. **Set Clear Goals**: Write down your goals and break them into smaller, manageable tasks. For example, if your goal is to get fit, start with setting a target to exercise for 30 minutes three times a week.

2. **Find Your Why**: Reflect on why your goals are important to you. Write down your reasons and revisit them whenever you feel your motivation waning.

3. **Create a Vision Board**: Gather images and words that

represent your goals and create a vision board. Place it somewhere you'll see it daily to remind yourself of what you're working towards.

4. **Reward Yourself**: Set up a reward system for yourself. For example, treat yourself to something you enjoy after completing a task or reaching a milestone.

5. **Stay Positive**: Practice positive self-talk and surround yourself with supportive people who encourage you to pursue your goals.

6. **Stay Accountable**: Find an accountability partner or join a group of like-minded individuals who can support and motivate you.

7. **Visualization**: Spend a few minutes each day visualizing yourself achieving your goals. Imagine the details of what it looks and feels like to succeed.

8. **Track Your Progress**: Keep a journal or use an app to track your progress towards your goals. Seeing how far you've come can boost your motivation to keep going.

The Impact of Motivation on Daily Life

Motivation can significantly impact various aspects of your daily life, from academics and career to personal growth and relationships. Here are some examples of how motivation can influence different areas:

- **Academic Success**: Motivated students tend to perform better academically. They are more likely to attend classes, complete assignments on time, and actively participate in learning activities.

- **Career Advancement**: In the workplace, motivated individuals are more productive, engaged, and likely to seek out opportunities for growth and development.

- **Personal Growth**: Motivation can drive you to pursue personal interests and hobbies, leading to a more fulfilling and balanced life.

- **Relationships**: Motivated individuals are more likely to invest time and effort into building and maintaining healthy relationships.

Personal Example: Jake, a university student, struggled with balancing his academic responsibilities and personal life. By setting clear goals and staying motivated, he managed to improve his grades, find time for his hobbies, and strengthen his relationships with friends and family.

Building Sustainable Motivation

Building sustainable motivation is an ongoing process. It requires regular practice and a positive mindset. Here are some additional tips to help you maintain motivation over the long term:

1. **Embrace Challenges**: View challenges as opportunities for growth rather than obstacles. Embracing challenges can keep you motivated and help you build resilience.

2. **Learn from Setbacks**: Setbacks are a natural part of any journey. Instead of getting discouraged, use setbacks as learning experiences to improve and move forward.

3. **Celebrate Progress**: Take time to celebrate your progress, no matter how small. Recognizing your achievements can boost your motivation and keep you focused on your goals.

4. **Stay Flexible**: Be open to adjusting your goals and strategies as needed. Staying flexible can help you adapt to changing circumstances and maintain your motivation.

5. **Seek Support**: Surround yourself with supportive people who encourage and motivate you. Sharing your goals with others can increase your commitment and motivation.

Conclusion

Motivation is a powerful force that can drive you to achieve your goals and lead a fulfilling life. By understanding the science behind motivation and implementing practical techniques, you can harness this energy and stay motivated even when facing challenges. In the next chapter, we'll explore empathy and how developing this skill can enhance your relationships and overall emotional intelligence.

5

EMPATHY

Introduction

Hey there! In the last chapter, we discussed motivation and how it drives you to achieve your goals. Now, let's explore another crucial component of Emotional Intelligence (EI): empathy. Empathy is the ability to understand and share the feelings of others. It's about stepping into someone else's shoes and experiencing their emotions. In this chapter, we'll delve into what empathy is, why it's important, and how you can develop this skill to enhance your relationships and overall emotional intelligence.

Understanding Empathy

Empathy involves recognizing and understanding the emotions of others. It goes beyond just hearing someone's words; it's about feeling their emotions and responding with compassion. There are three main types of empathy:

1. **Cognitive Empathy**: This is understanding someone's

thoughts and emotions from a rational perspective. It's about knowing how they feel and what they might be thinking.

2. **Emotional Empathy**: This is feeling someone else's emotions as if they were your own. It's about sharing their emotional experience.

3. **Compassionate Empathy**: This goes beyond understanding and feeling; it involves taking action to help someone in need.

Imagine your friend just failed an important exam. Cognitive empathy helps you understand their disappointment, emotional empathy allows you to feel their sadness, and compassionate empathy drives you to comfort them and offer support.

Benefits of Empathy

Empathy offers numerous benefits, including:

- **Stronger Relationships**: Empathy helps you build deeper, more meaningful connections with others.

- **Better Communication**: Understanding others' emotions can improve your ability to communicate effectively.

- **Conflict Resolution**: Empathy allows you to see different perspectives, making it easier to resolve conflicts.

- **Increased Compassion**: Being empathetic makes you more compassionate and caring towards others.

Personal Example: Think about Sarah, who noticed her friend Jenna was unusually quiet and withdrawn. Instead of ignoring it, Sarah asked Jenna how she was feeling. Jenna opened up about her recent breakup, and Sarah listened with empathy, offering her support. This deepened their friendship and helped Jenna feel understood and less alone.

Techniques to Develop Empathy

Developing empathy takes practice and conscious effort. Here are some techniques to help you get started:

1. **Active Listening**: Truly listen to what others are saying without interrupting or planning your response.

   - **Detailed Practice**: When someone is speaking, focus entirely on them. Maintain eye contact, nod, and provide verbal affirmations like "I see" or "That sounds tough." Reflect on what they've said by summarizing their points to show you understand.

2. **Perspective-Taking**: Try to see situations from others' perspectives.

   - **Detailed Practice**: When in a conversation or conflict, pause and ask yourself how the other person might be feeling and why. Consider their background, experiences, and current situation to understand their point of view.

3. **Emotional Mimicry**: Mirror the emotions of others to connect more deeply.

- **Detailed Practice**: Pay attention to the emotions expressed by others and allow yourself to feel them. If someone is excited, share in their excitement. If they're sad, let yourself feel a bit of their sadness to understand them better.

4. **Practice Compassion**: Engage in acts of kindness and compassion regularly.

- **Detailed Practice**: Volunteer for causes you care about, offer help to someone in need, or simply be there for a friend. These actions can enhance your ability to empathize by putting you in others' shoes.

5. **Mindfulness**: Being present in the moment can enhance your ability to empathize.

- **Detailed Practice**: Practice mindfulness by focusing on your breath, sensations, and surroundings. This helps you stay present and fully engage with others' emotions when interacting with them.

Personal Stories and Examples

Personal stories can make the concept of empathy more relatable. Let's look at some examples:

Alex's Journey: Building Empathy through Volunteering

Step 1: Recognizing the Need for Empathy

Alex, a college student, realized that he wanted to become more empathetic. He often found it challenging to understand the struggles of others and felt that enhancing his empathy skills would help him build better relationships.

- **Self-Awareness**: The first step for Alex was acknowledging his desire to improve his empathy. He recognized that understanding and connecting with others on a deeper level was important for his personal growth.

Step 2: Choosing to Volunteer

To develop his empathy, Alex decided to volunteer at a local shelter. He believed that interacting with people facing difficult circumstances would provide him with valuable insights and experiences.

- **Taking Action**: Alex contacted a nearby shelter and signed up as a volunteer. He committed to spending a few hours each week helping out and getting to know the people there.

Step 3: Active Listening and Understanding

At the shelter, Alex met various individuals with different backgrounds and stories. One day, he met a man named John, who had recently lost his job and home. Alex made a conscious effort to listen actively to John's story without interrupting or judging.

- **Active Listening**: Alex focused entirely on John, maintaining eye contact and nodding to show that he was engaged. He asked open-ended questions to encourage John to share more about his experiences and feelings.

Step 4: Feeling and Offering Support

As John shared his struggles, Alex didn't just hear his words; he felt his pain. He imagined what it must be like to be in John's situation, which helped him connect on an emotional level.

- **Empathy in Action**: Alex expressed his empathy by saying, "I can't imagine how tough this must be for you. Is there anything specific I can do to help?" He offered genuine support, which made John feel understood and valued.

Step 5: Reflecting on the Experience

Volunteering at the shelter and interacting with people like John helped Alex develop deeper empathy and compassion. He reflected on his experiences and how they had changed his perspective.

- **Reflection**: Alex kept a journal where he wrote about his volunteering experiences, the people he met, and what he learned from them. This reflection helped him internalize the importance of empathy and reinforced his commitment to being more empathetic in his daily life.

Through volunteering at the shelter, Alex successfully built his empathy skills. By recognizing the need for empathy, choosing to volunteer, actively listening, feeling and offering support, and reflecting on his experiences, Alex developed a deeper understanding of others' struggles and learned to connect with them on a more compassionate level.

Maria's Experience: Empathy in the Workplace

Step 1: Observing a Colleague's Struggles

Maria, a recent college graduate, started her first job at a marketing firm. She quickly noticed that one of her colleagues, Lisa, seemed stressed and overwhelmed. Maria wanted to help but wasn't sure how to approach the situation.

- **Observation**: Maria paid attention to Lisa's behavior and body language. She noticed that Lisa often looked tired, seemed distracted during meetings, and occasionally appeared upset.

Step 2: Reaching Out with Empathy

Instead of ignoring Lisa's struggles, Maria decided to approach her with empathy. She believed that understanding Lisa's perspective would help her offer meaningful support.

- **Taking Action**: Maria approached Lisa during a break and said, "Hey Lisa, you seem a bit stressed lately. Is everything okay? I'm here if you want to talk." This simple act of reaching out showed Lisa that Maria cared and was willing to listen.

Step 3: Active Listening and Offering Support

Lisa opened up to Maria about her heavy workload and personal issues. Maria listened empathetically, giving Lisa her full attention and acknowledging her feelings.

- **Active Listening**: Maria made sure not to interrupt Lisa and provided verbal affirmations like "I understand" and "That sounds really tough." She also asked open-ended questions to encourage Lisa to share more about her struggles.

Step 4: Providing Practical Help

After listening to Lisa's concerns, Maria offered to help with some of her tasks. She believed that taking some of the workload off Lisa's shoulders would alleviate her stress and show her that she wasn't alone.

- **Empathy in Action**: Maria said, "I know you have a lot on your plate. How about we tackle some of these tasks together? I'm happy to help with whatever I can." This practical support made a significant difference for Lisa and demonstrated Maria's empathy.

Step 5: Building a Stronger Professional Relationship

Maria's act of empathy not only helped Lisa but also strengthened their professional relationship. Lisa felt valued and supported, which improved their teamwork and collaboration.

- **Strengthened Bonds**: Over time, Maria and Lisa developed a strong working relationship based on mutual respect and understanding. They supported each other through challenging projects and celebrated their successes together.

Through her empathetic actions, Maria significantly improved her relationship with Lisa and contributed to a more supportive work environment. By observing her colleague's struggles, reaching out with empathy, actively listening, providing practical help, and building a stronger professional relationship, Maria exemplified the power of empathy in the workplace.

The Science Behind Empathy

Empathy isn't just a feel-good concept; it has a strong scientific foundation. Research shows that empathy is linked to various positive outcomes, including better mental health, enhanced social connections, and improved leadership skills.

Studies and Data:

- **Empathy and the Brain**: Neuroscience research has shown that empathy activates specific areas of the brain, such as the anterior insula and the anterior cingulate cortex. These areas are involved in processing emotions and understanding others' feelings (Decety, J., & Jackson, P.

L., 2004).

- **Empathy and Social Connections**: A study published in the journal *Emotion* found that people with high levels of empathy tend to have stronger social connections and better relationships. This is because empathy fosters understanding and trust (Morelli, S.A., Lieberman, M.D., & Zaki, J., 2015).

- **Empathy and Leadership**: Research from the Center for Creative Leadership indicates that empathetic leaders are more effective. They are better at building trust, resolving conflicts, and creating a positive work environment (Gentry, W.A., Weber, T.J., & Sadri, G., 2007).

Practical Exercises

Here are some practical exercises to help you develop empathy:

1. **Active Listening**: Truly listen to what others are saying without interrupting or planning your response. Focus entirely on them, maintain eye contact, nod, and provide verbal affirmations like "I see" or "That sounds tough." Reflect on what they've said by summarizing their points to show you understand.

2. **Perspective-Taking**: Try to see situations from others' perspectives. When in a conversation or conflict, pause and ask yourself how the other person might be feeling

and why. Consider their background, experiences, and current situation to understand their point of view.

3. **Emotional Mimicry**: Mirror the emotions of others to connect more deeply. Pay attention to the emotions expressed by others and allow yourself to feel them. If someone is excited, share in their excitement. If they're sad, let yourself feel a bit of their sadness to understand them better.

4. **Practice Compassion**: Engage in acts of kindness and compassion regularly. Volunteer for causes you care about, offer help to someone in need, or simply be there for a friend. These actions can enhance your ability to empathize by putting you in others' shoes.

5. **Mindfulness**: Being present in the moment can enhance your ability to empathize. Practice mindfulness by focusing on your breath, sensations, and surroundings. This helps you stay present and fully engage with others' emotions when interacting with them.

6. **Reading Fiction**: Reading books that explore characters' inner lives and emotions can improve your ability to empathize. Choose novels that provide deep insights into the characters' thoughts and feelings.

7. **Empathy Journaling**: Keep a journal where you reflect on your interactions with others. Write about what you

observed, how you felt, and what you learned about the other person's emotions.

The Impact of Empathy on Daily Life

Empathy can significantly impact various aspects of your daily life, from personal relationships to professional interactions. Here are some examples of how empathy can influence different areas:

- **Personal Relationships**: Empathy allows you to connect more deeply with friends and family. It helps you understand their feelings and respond with care and compassion.

- **Professional Success**: In the workplace, empathy can enhance teamwork, improve communication, and build stronger relationships with colleagues and clients.

- **Conflict Resolution**: Empathy helps you see conflicts from different perspectives, making it easier to find mutually beneficial solutions.

- **Mental Health**: Empathetic individuals tend to have better mental health because they feel more connected and supported by others.

Personal Example: Jake, a university student, noticed that his roommate, Mike, was acting distant and irritable. Instead of getting annoyed, Jake approached Mike with empathy. He asked if everything was okay and listened without judgment. Mike opened up about his struggles with family issues, and Jake offered his support. This empathetic approach not only strengthened their friendship but also helped Mike feel understood and less alone.

Building Sustainable Empathy

Building sustainable empathy is an ongoing process that requires regular practice and a genuine interest in understanding others. Here are some additional tips to help you maintain empathy over the long term:

1. **Stay Curious**: Cultivate a genuine interest in others' lives and experiences. Ask questions and seek to understand their perspectives.

2. **Practice Patience**: Empathy requires patience. Take the time to listen and understand others without rushing to judgment or solutions.

3. **Reflect on Your Experiences**: Regularly reflect on your interactions with others and consider how you can improve your empathetic responses.

4. **Seek Diverse Perspectives**: Engage with people from different backgrounds and cultures to broaden your understanding and appreciation of diverse experiences.

5. **Practice Self-Compassion**: Being kind and empathetic to yourself can enhance your ability to empathize with

others. Recognize your own emotions and treat yourself with the same compassion you offer to others.

Conclusion

Empathy is a powerful skill that can enhance your relationships, improve your communication, and foster a deeper understanding of others. By developing empathy, you can build stronger connections and create a more compassionate and supportive environment. In the next chapter, we'll explore social skills and how mastering these skills can further enhance your emotional intelligence and overall success.

6

SOCIAL SKILLS

Introduction

Hey there! In the last chapter, we explored empathy and how it can enhance your relationships and emotional intelligence. Now, let's dive into the final key component of Emotional Intelligence (EI): social skills. Social skills are the tools we use to interact with others effectively. They help us communicate, build relationships, and navigate social situations with ease. In this chapter, we'll discuss what social skills are, why they're important, and how you can develop these skills to succeed in both personal and professional settings.

Understanding Social Skills

Social skills encompass a wide range of abilities that allow you to interact harmoniously with others. These skills include communication, cooperation, conflict resolution, and leadership. Essentially, social skills help you build and maintain positive relationships, work well in teams, and handle social interactions smoothly.

Imagine you're at a party where you don't know many people. Social skills help you start conversations, make new friends, and enjoy the event. They enable you to read social cues, understand others' perspectives, and respond appropriately in different situations.

Benefits of Social Skills

Having strong social skills offers numerous benefits, including:

- **Enhanced Relationships**: Social skills help you build and maintain meaningful relationships with friends, family, and colleagues.

- **Improved Communication**: Good social skills enable you to express yourself clearly and understand others effectively.

- **Better Conflict Resolution**: Social skills help you manage and resolve conflicts in a constructive manner.

- **Increased Career Success**: In the workplace, social skills are essential for teamwork, leadership, and career advancement.

Personal Example: Consider Emma, who started a new job at a marketing firm. She used her social skills to introduce herself to her colleagues, join team projects, and build positive relationships with her coworkers. Her ability to communicate effectively and work well with others quickly made her a valuable team member.

Techniques to Develop Social Skills

Developing social skills takes practice and a willingness to step out of your comfort zone. Here are some techniques to help you get started:

1. **Active Listening**: Pay full attention to the speaker, show that you're listening, and respond thoughtfully.

   - **Detailed Practice**: When someone is speaking, focus entirely on them. Maintain eye contact, nod, and provide verbal affirmations like "I see" or "That makes sense." Avoid interrupting and wait until they finish before responding.

2. **Effective Communication**: Use clear and concise language, and be mindful of your tone and body language.

   - **Detailed Practice**: Practice expressing your thoughts and feelings clearly. Pay attention to your body language and tone of voice, as they can convey as much as your words. Make sure your non-verbal cues match your verbal messages.

3. **Empathy in Action**: Apply your empathy skills to understand and respond to others' emotions.

- **Detailed Practice**: When interacting with others, try to put yourself in their shoes. Reflect on their feelings and perspectives before responding. Show understanding and compassion in your responses.

4. **Conflict Resolution**: Approach conflicts with a calm and constructive attitude, seeking mutually beneficial solutions.

   - **Detailed Practice**: When a conflict arises, take a deep breath and approach the situation calmly. Listen to the other person's perspective and express your own feelings without blame. Work together to find a solution that satisfies both parties.

5. **Networking**: Build a network of contacts by attending social events, joining clubs, and participating in online communities.

   - **Detailed Practice**: Take opportunities to meet new people, both in-person and online. Attend events related to your interests, join clubs or groups, and engage in conversations. Follow up with new contacts to build lasting relationships.

6. **Assertiveness**: Express your needs and opinions confidently and respectfully.

   - **Detailed Practice**: Practice assertive communication

by expressing your needs and opinions clearly and respectfully. Use "I" statements to take ownership of your feelings and avoid blaming others. For example, say "I feel upset when..." instead of "You make me upset by...".

Personal Stories and Examples

Personal stories can make the concept of social skills more relatable. Let's look at some examples:

Alex's Journey: Building Confidence in Social Settings

Alex, a college student, felt anxious in social settings and struggled to make new friends. Determined to improve, he started by attending small social events on campus. He practiced active listening and effective communication, which helped him engage in meaningful conversations. Over time, Alex built his confidence and expanded his social circle, making lasting friendships.

Maria's Experience: Navigating Workplace Dynamics

Maria, a recent college graduate, found her first job challenging due to office politics and different personalities. She decided to focus on developing her social skills to navigate these dynamics better. By practicing empathy, effective communication, and conflict resolution, Maria improved her relationships with colleagues and became known for her collaborative approach. Her social skills not only made her work environment more pleasant but also opened up new opportunities for career advancement.

The Science Behind Social Skills

Social skills aren't just about being friendly; they have a strong scientific foundation. Research shows that social skills are linked to various positive outcomes, including better mental health, improved relationships, and greater career success.

Studies and Data:

- **Social Skills and Mental Health**: A study published in the journal *PLOS ONE* found that individuals with strong social skills tend to have better mental health and well-being. Social interactions provide emotional support, reduce stress, and enhance life satisfaction (Segrin, C., & Taylor, M., 2007).

- **Social Skills and Relationship Satisfaction**: Research from the University of Arizona indicates that social skills are crucial for maintaining satisfying and healthy relationships. Effective communication and empathy contribute to relationship quality and longevity (Segrin, C., & Flora, J., 2000).

- **Social Skills and Career Success**: A study from Harvard University, the Carnegie Foundation, and Stanford Research Center found that 85% of job success comes from having well-developed soft skills, including social skills, while only 15% comes from technical skills (Robles, M.M., 2012).

Practical Exercises

Here are some practical exercises to help you develop social skills:

1. **Active Listening**: Pay full attention to the speaker, show that you're listening, and respond thoughtfully. When someone is speaking, focus entirely on them. Maintain eye contact, nod, and provide verbal affirmations like "I see" or "That makes sense." Avoid interrupting and wait until they finish before responding.

2. **Effective Communication**: Use clear and concise language, and be mindful of your tone and body language. Practice expressing your thoughts and feelings clearly. Pay attention to your body language and tone of voice, as they can convey as much as your words. Make sure your non-verbal cues match your verbal messages.

3. **Empathy in Action**: Apply your empathy skills to understand and respond to others' emotions. When interacting with others, try to put yourself in their shoes. Reflect on their feelings and perspectives before responding. Show understanding and compassion in your responses.

4. **Conflict Resolution**: Approach conflicts with a calm and constructive attitude, seeking mutually beneficial solutions. When a conflict arises, take a deep breath and

approach the situation calmly. Listen to the other person's perspective and express your own feelings without blame. Work together to find a solution that satisfies both parties.

5. **Networking**: Build a network of contacts by attending social events, joining clubs, and participating in online communities. Take opportunities to meet new people, both in-person and online. Attend events related to your interests, join clubs or groups, and engage in conversations. Follow up with new contacts to build lasting relationships.

6. **Assertiveness**: Express your needs and opinions confidently and respectfully. Practice assertive communication by expressing your needs and opinions clearly and respectfully. Use "I" statements to take ownership of your feelings and avoid blaming others. For example, say "I feel upset when..." instead of "You make me upset by...".

7. **Role-Playing**: Practice social interactions and scenarios through role-playing. Partner with a friend or mentor to simulate different social situations, such as job interviews, networking events, or conflict resolution. This can help you gain confidence and refine your social skills.

8. **Public Speaking**: Improve your communication skills by practicing public speaking. Join a public speaking group like Toastmasters, or practice speaking in front of a mirror

or with friends. This can help you become more comfortable and articulate in social situations.

The Impact of Social Skills on Daily Life

Social skills can significantly impact various aspects of your daily life, from personal relationships to professional interactions. Here are some examples of how social skills can influence different areas:

- **Personal Relationships**: Social skills help you connect more deeply with friends and family, enhancing the quality of your relationships.

- **Professional Success**: In the workplace, social skills are essential for teamwork, leadership, and career advancement.

- **Conflict Resolution**: Social skills enable you to manage and resolve conflicts constructively, leading to healthier interactions.

- **Mental Health**: Strong social skills contribute to better mental health by providing emotional support and reducing feelings of isolation.

Personal Example: Jake, a university student, struggled with making friends and participating in group projects. By developing his social skills, he became more confident in starting conversations and collaborating with others. This not only improved his academic performance but also enriched his social life, making him feel more connected and supported.

Building Sustainable Social Skills

Building sustainable social skills is an ongoing process that requires regular practice and a genuine interest in connecting with others. Here are some additional tips to help you maintain and enhance your social skills over the long term:

1. **Practice Regularly**: Like any skill, social skills improve with practice. Engage in social interactions regularly to keep your skills sharp.

2. **Seek Feedback**: Ask friends, family, or colleagues for feedback on your social interactions. Use their input to identify areas for improvement.

3. **Stay Open-Minded**: Be open to new experiences and different perspectives. Embrace diversity and seek to understand people from various backgrounds.

4. **Reflect on Your Interactions**: Regularly reflect on your social interactions and consider what went well and what could be improved. Use this reflection to refine your approach.

5. **Stay Positive**: Maintain a positive attitude and approach social interactions with optimism and enthusiasm. Positive energy is contagious and can enhance your social

connections.

Conclusion

Social skills are essential tools that can enhance your relationships, improve your communication, and help you navigate social situations with ease. By developing these skills, you can build stronger connections, succeed in your personal and professional life, and create a more supportive and compassionate environment. In the next chapter, we'll explore how to integrate all the components of emotional intelligence to achieve overall well-being and success.

7

Integrating Emotional Intelligence for Overall Well-Being

Introduction

We've covered a lot in the previous chapters about the individual components of Emotional Intelligence (EI): self-awareness, self-regulation, motivation, empathy, and social skills. Now, let's bring it all together and discuss how integrating these components can help you achieve overall well-being and success. In this chapter, we'll explore what it means to integrate emotional intelligence, why it's important, and how you can apply it to various aspects of your life.

Understanding Integration of Emotional Intelligence

Integrating emotional intelligence means using the skills we've discussed in harmony to navigate life's challenges, build meaningful relationships, and achieve personal and professional goals. Think of it as a toolkit where each component plays a crucial role in helping you handle different situations effectively.

Imagine you're at a new job and feeling overwhelmed. Self-awareness helps you recognize your stress, self-regulation helps you stay calm, motivation keeps you focused on your goals, empathy helps you understand your colleagues' perspectives, and social skills help you communicate effectively. By integrating these components, you can manage the situation better and thrive in your new role.

Benefits of Integrating Emotional Intelligence

Integrating emotional intelligence offers numerous benefits, including:

- **Enhanced Resilience**: You can bounce back from setbacks more easily by understanding and managing your emotions.

- **Better Relationships**: Integrated EI helps you build deeper, more meaningful connections with others.

- **Improved Decision-Making**: You can make more informed and balanced decisions by considering both your emotions and logical reasoning.

- **Greater Well-Being**: Overall, integrating EI leads to improved mental health, increased happiness, and greater life satisfaction.

Personal Example: Consider Emma, who uses her emotional intelligence skills daily. When she faces a stressful situation at work, she uses self-awareness to identify her feelings, self-regulation to stay calm, motivation to stay focused on her tasks, empathy to understand her team's concerns, and social skills to communicate effectively. This holistic approach helps Emma maintain her well-being and succeed in her role.

Techniques to Integrate Emotional Intelligence

Integrating emotional intelligence requires practice and intentionality. Here are some techniques to help you get started:

1. **Mindfulness Practice**: Regular mindfulness practice can enhance all components of EI by keeping you present and aware.

   - **Detailed Practice**: Dedicate 10-15 minutes each day to mindfulness meditation. Sit comfortably, close your eyes, and focus on your breath. This practice can help you stay calm, recognize your emotions, and respond thoughtfully to various situations.

2. **Reflective Journaling**: Writing down your thoughts and feelings can help you understand and integrate your emotional experiences.

   - **Detailed Practice**: At the end of each day, reflect on your interactions and decisions. Write about how you used each component of EI and how it impacted the outcomes. Over time, this practice can help you see patterns and areas for improvement.

3. **Goal Setting with EI**: Set goals that involve using all components of EI.

   - **Detailed Practice**: For example, if you want to improve your relationships, set specific goals like practicing active listening (social skills), understanding your emotions (self-awareness), and showing empathy. Break these goals into smaller, actionable steps and track your progress.

4. **Seek Feedback**: Regularly ask for feedback from friends, family, and colleagues to gain insights into your use of EI.

   - **Detailed Practice**: Approach trusted individuals and ask for honest feedback about your emotional intelligence. Reflect on their input and identify areas where you can improve. Use this feedback to refine your approach.

5. **Role-Playing**: Practice integrating EI through role-playing scenarios.

   - **Detailed Practice**: Partner with a friend or mentor to simulate different situations, such as handling conflicts or giving presentations. Practice using all components of EI to navigate these scenarios effectively.

Personal Stories and Examples

Personal stories can make the concept of integrating emotional intelligence more relatable. Let's look at some examples:

Alex's Journey: Balancing School and Personal Life

Alex, a college student, struggled to balance his academic responsibilities with his personal life. By integrating emotional intelligence, he managed to find a better balance. He used self-awareness to recognize when he was feeling overwhelmed, self-regulation to manage his stress, motivation to stay focused on his studies, empathy to understand his friends' needs, and social skills to communicate his boundaries. This holistic approach helped Alex maintain his well-being and improve his relationships.

Maria's Experience: Navigating a Career Transition

Maria, a recent college graduate, decided to switch careers from marketing to graphic design. The transition was challenging, but by integrating emotional intelligence, she managed to navigate it successfully. She used self-awareness to identify her passion for design, self-regulation to handle the stress of learning new skills, motivation to stay committed to her goals, empathy to understand her new colleagues' perspectives, and social skills to build a network in her new field. This integration of EI helped Maria thrive in her new career.

The Science Behind Integrating Emotional Intelligence

Integrating emotional intelligence isn't just a feel-good concept; it has a strong scientific foundation. Research shows that individuals who effectively integrate EI tend to have better mental health, improved relationships, and greater professional success.

Studies and Data:

- **Emotional Intelligence and Mental Health**: A study published in the *Journal of Personality and Social Psychology* found that individuals with high EI tend to have lower levels of stress and anxiety, leading to better overall mental health (Salovey, P., & Mayer, J.D., 1990).

- **Emotional Intelligence and Leadership**: Research from Harvard Business School indicates that leaders with high EI are more effective. They are better at managing teams, making decisions, and driving organizational success (Goleman, D., 1998).

- **Emotional Intelligence and Academic Performance**: A study published in *Frontiers in Psychology* found that students with high EI tend to perform better academically. This is because they can manage their emotions, stay motivated, and build positive relationships with peers and teachers (Mavroveli, S., & Sánchez-Ruiz, M.J., 2011).

Practical Exercises

Here are some practical exercises to help you integrate emotional intelligence into your daily life:

1. **Mindfulness Practice**: Dedicate 10-15 minutes each day to mindfulness meditation. Sit comfortably, close your eyes, and focus on your breath. This practice can help you stay calm, recognize your emotions, and respond thoughtfully to various situations.

2. **Reflective Journaling**: At the end of each day, reflect on your interactions and decisions. Write about how you used each component of EI and how it impacted the outcomes. Over time, this practice can help you see patterns and areas for improvement.

3. **Goal Setting with EI**: Set goals that involve using all components of EI. For example, if you want to improve your relationships, set specific goals like practicing active listening (social skills), understanding your emotions (self-awareness), and showing empathy. Break these goals into smaller, actionable steps and track your progress.

4. **Seek Feedback**: Approach trusted individuals and ask for honest feedback about your emotional intelligence. Reflect on their input and identify areas where you can improve. Use this feedback to refine your approach.

5. **Role-Playing**: Partner with a friend or mentor to sim-

ulate different situations, such as handling conflicts or giving presentations. Practice using all components of EI to navigate these scenarios effectively.

6. **Visualization**: Spend a few minutes each day visualizing yourself successfully integrating emotional intelligence into different aspects of your life. Imagine how you will use self-awareness, self-regulation, motivation, empathy, and social skills to handle various situations.

The Impact of Integrating Emotional Intelligence on Daily Life

Integrating emotional intelligence can significantly impact various aspects of your daily life, from personal relationships to professional success. Here are some examples of how EI integration can influence different areas:

- **Personal Relationships**: By integrating EI, you can build deeper and more meaningful relationships with friends and family. Understanding your emotions and those of others helps you connect on a deeper level and resolve conflicts more effectively.

- **Professional Success**: In the workplace, integrating EI can enhance teamwork, improve leadership skills, and boost career advancement. You can navigate office dynamics, handle stress, and build a positive work environment.

- **Academic Performance**: For students, integrating EI can lead to better academic performance. Managing emotions, staying motivated, and building positive relationships with peers and teachers contribute to a more successful academic experience.

- **Mental Health**: Overall, integrating EI leads to better mental health. It helps you manage stress, build resilience, and maintain a positive outlook on life.

Personal Example: Jake, a university student, found that integrating emotional intelligence into his daily life made a significant difference. He used self-awareness to recognize when he needed a break, self-regulation to stay calm during exams, motivation to keep pushing towards his goals, empathy to understand his roommates' perspectives, and social skills to build a supportive network of friends. This holistic approach helped Jake maintain his well-being and succeed academically.

Building Sustainable Emotional Intelligence Integration

Building sustainable emotional intelligence integration is an ongoing process that requires regular practice and a genuine interest in personal growth. Here are some additional tips to help you maintain and enhance your EI integration over the long term:

1. **Stay Committed**: Regularly practice the techniques and exercises discussed in this chapter. Consistency is key to developing and maintaining strong EI integration.

2. **Reflect and Adjust**: Regularly reflect on your progress and adjust your strategies as needed. Stay open to learning and growth.

3. **Seek Support**: Surround yourself with supportive people who encourage and motivate you to integrate EI into your life.

4. **Celebrate Successes**: Take time to celebrate your successes and milestones. Recognizing your achievements can boost your motivation and reinforce positive behavior.

5. **Stay Curious**: Cultivate a genuine interest in understanding yourself and others. Stay curious about your emotions and the emotions of those around you.

Conclusion

Integrating emotional intelligence is a powerful way to enhance your overall well-being and achieve success in various aspects of your life. By combining self-awareness, self-regulation, motivation, empathy, and social skills, you can navigate life's challenges with greater ease and build more meaningful connections. In the next chapter, we'll explore practical applications of emotional intelligence in different areas of life, including personal relationships, academics, and professional settings.

8

EMOTIONAL INTELLIGENCE IN ROMANTIC RELATIONSHIPS

Introduction

In the previous chapters, we've explored various components of Emotional Intelligence (EI) and how they can enhance different aspects of your life. Now, let's focus on applying these principles to improve your romantic relationships. Romantic relationships are a significant part of life, and using EI can help you build deeper emotional connections, navigate challenges, and foster a more loving and supportive partnership. In this chapter, we'll discuss how to apply EI in romantic relationships, enhance emotional connections with your partner, and overcome common relationship challenges through EI.

Understanding Emotional Intelligence in Romantic Relationships

Emotional Intelligence in romantic relationships involves using self-awareness, self-regulation, motivation, empathy, and social skills to understand and connect with your partner on a deeper level. It's about recognizing and managing your emotions and those of your partner to create a harmonious and fulfilling relationship.

Imagine you're disagreeing with your partner about plans for the weekend. Using EI, you can recognize your frustration (self-awareness), stay calm and avoid snapping (self-regulation), remember your commitment to a happy relationship (motivation), understand your partner's perspective (empathy), and communicate effectively to find a compromise (social skills).

Benefits of Emotional Intelligence in Romantic Relationships

Applying EI in your romantic relationships offers numerous benefits, including:

- **Stronger Emotional Connection**: EI helps you understand and connect with your partner's emotions, leading to a deeper emotional bond.

- **Better Communication**: Effective use of EI enhances communication, reducing misunderstandings and conflicts.

- **Improved Conflict Resolution**: EI allows you to approach conflicts calmly and constructively, leading to healthier resolutions.

- **Increased Relationship Satisfaction**: Couples with high EI tend to have more satisfying and fulfilling relationships.

Personal Example: Consider Emma and Jake, a couple who used EI to strengthen their relationship. When they faced disagreements, they applied self-awareness to recognize their emotions, self-regulation to stay calm, empathy to understand each other's perspectives, and social skills to communicate effectively. This approach helped them navigate challenges and build a stronger, more loving relationship.

Techniques to Apply EI in Romantic Relationships

Developing and applying EI in your romantic relationship requires practice and intentional effort. Here are some techniques to help you get started:

1. **Practice Active Listening**: Truly listen to your partner without interrupting or planning your response.

    - **Detailed Practice**: When your partner is speaking, give them your full attention. Maintain eye contact, nod, and provide verbal affirmations like "I understand" or "That must be difficult." Reflect back what they've said to show you understand, such as "So, you're feeling upset because..."

2. **Express Your Emotions Clearly**: Use "I" statements to

express your feelings without blaming your partner.

- **Detailed Practice**: Instead of saying "You never listen to me," say "I feel unheard when I try to share my thoughts with you." This approach helps you take ownership of your emotions and reduces defensiveness.

3. **Show Empathy**: Understand and validate your partner's feelings, even if you don't agree with them.

- **Detailed Practice**: If your partner is upset about something, try to understand their perspective. Say things like, "I can see why you're feeling that way" or "It sounds like that really bothered you."

4. **Manage Your Stress**: Use self-regulation techniques to stay calm during conflicts.

- **Detailed Practice**: When you feel yourself getting upset, take a few deep breaths, count to ten, or take a short break to cool down. This helps you approach the situation more calmly and rationally.

5. **Set Relationship Goals**: Work together to set goals for your relationship, such as spending more quality time together or improving communication.

- **Detailed Practice**: Sit down with your partner and

discuss your relationship goals. Write them down and create a plan to achieve them. Regularly check in on your progress and celebrate your successes together.

6. **Practice Forgiveness**: Let go of grudges and focus on moving forward.

   ○ **Detailed Practice**: When conflicts arise, focus on resolving the issue rather than assigning blame. After a disagreement, discuss what you can learn from the experience and how you can prevent similar issues in the future. Practice letting go of resentment and forgiving your partner.

Alex and Maria's Journey: Navigating Relationship Challenges

Alex and Maria, a couple who had been dating for a year, faced challenges in their relationship due to busy schedules and miscommunications. By applying EI, they were able to improve their relationship significantly. Here's a detailed look at the steps they took:

1. **Identifying the Problem**: Both Alex and Maria felt that their busy schedules were causing them to drift apart. They often miscommunicated about plans, leading to frustration and misunderstandings.

2. **Practicing Active Listening**: They decided to practice active listening to improve their communication. When Maria felt overwhelmed by her workload, Alex made an effort to listen without interrupting. He maintained eye contact, nodded, and provided verbal affirmations like "I understand that you're feeling stressed."

3. **Expressing Emotions Clearly**: They worked on expressing their emotions clearly using "I" statements. Instead of accusing each other, they shared their feelings. For example, Alex would say, "I feel frustrated when we don't spend time together," instead of "You never make time for me."

4. **Showing Empathy**: Alex made a conscious effort to understand Maria's perspective. When Maria shared her stress about work, Alex validated her feelings by saying, "I can see why you're feeling overwhelmed. It sounds really challenging."

5. **Setting Relationship Goals**: They set goals to spend more quality time together. They planned regular date nights and scheduled time for each other despite their busy schedules. They also set a goal to check in with each other daily about how they were feeling.

6. **Managing Stress Together**: They practiced self-regulation techniques to manage stress during conflicts. When

disagreements arose, they took breaks to cool down and then came back to discuss the issue calmly.

7. **Practicing Forgiveness**: They made a commitment to let go of past grudges and focus on moving forward. After conflicts, they discussed what they could learn from the experience and how to avoid similar issues in the future.

These steps helped Alex and Maria improve their communication, strengthen their emotional connection, and build a more supportive relationship.

Emma and Jake's Experience: Building a Stronger Emotional Connection

Emma and Jake, who had been together for three years, wanted to deepen their emotional connection. They decided to set relationship goals, such as having weekly date nights and practicing mindfulness together. Here's a detailed look at the steps they took:

1. **Setting Relationship Goals**: They sat down together and discussed what they wanted to achieve in their relationship. They decided to have weekly date nights to spend quality time together and practice mindfulness to stay connected.

2. **Weekly Date Nights**: They scheduled a specific night each week for a date. They took turns planning the dates, which ranged from dinner out to watching a movie at

home or trying a new activity together. This regular time together helped them reconnect and enjoy each other's company.

3. **Practicing Mindfulness Together**: They incorporated mindfulness practices into their routine. Every morning, they spent ten minutes meditating together. This practice helped them stay present and connected throughout the day.

4. **Managing Stress During Conflicts**: They worked on managing their stress during conflicts by taking breaks and using self-regulation techniques. If a disagreement became heated, they agreed to take a short break, cool down, and then come back to discuss the issue calmly.

5. **Active Listening**: They made a conscious effort to practice active listening. During their weekly check-ins, they listened to each other without interrupting and reflected back what the other person said to show understanding.

6. **Expressing Emotions Clearly**: They used "I" statements to express their feelings without blaming each other. For example, Emma would say, "I feel hurt when you don't call if you're going to be late," instead of "You never call when you're late."

7. **Showing Empathy**: They practiced empathy by validating each other's feelings. When Jake shared his stress

about work, Emma responded with empathy, saying, "I understand that you're under a lot of pressure. Let's figure out how we can make things easier for you at home."

8. **Regular Check-Ins**: They scheduled regular check-ins to discuss their relationship and any issues that may have arisen. During these check-ins, they expressed their feelings, listened to each other, and discussed ways to improve their relationship.

These efforts helped Emma and Jake build a stronger emotional connection, improve their communication, and enhance their overall relationship satisfaction.

The Science Behind Emotional Intelligence in Romantic Relationships

Applying emotional intelligence in romantic relationships isn't just a feel-good concept; it has a strong scientific foundation. Research shows that couples with high EI tend to have better communication, stronger emotional bonds, and greater relationship satisfaction.

Studies and Data:

- **Emotional Intelligence and Relationship Satisfaction**: A study published in the *Journal of Social and Personal Relationships* found that couples with high EI have higher levels of relationship satisfaction. This is because they can manage their emotions, empathize with their partners, and communicate effectively (Brackett, M.A., Warner, R.M., & Bosco, J.S., 2005).

- **Emotional Intelligence and Conflict Resolution**: Research from the *Journal of Marriage and Family* indicates that couples with high EI are better at resolving conflicts. They approach disagreements with empathy and understanding, leading to healthier and more constructive resolutions (Gottman, J.M., & Silver, N., 1999).

- **Emotional Intelligence and Emotional Connection**: A study published in *Emotion* found that emotional intelligence enhances emotional connection between partners. Couples who understand and manage their emotions are better able to connect on a deeper level (Zeidner, M., Matthews, G., & Roberts, R.D., 2012).

Practical Exercises

Here are some practical exercises to help you apply emotional intelligence in your romantic relationship:

1. **Active Listening**: Truly listen to your partner without interrupting or planning your response. Give them your full attention, maintain eye contact, nod, and provide verbal affirmations like "I understand" or "That must be difficult." Reflect back what they've said to show you understand, such as "So, you're feeling upset because..."

2. **Express Your Emotions Clearly**: Use "I" statements to express your feelings without blaming your partner. Instead of saying "You never listen to me," say "I feel unheard when I try to share my thoughts with you." This approach helps you take ownership of your emotions and reduces defensiveness.

3. **Show Empathy**: Understand and validate your partner's feelings, even if you don't agree with them. If your partner is upset about something, try to understand their perspective. Say things like, "I can see why you're feeling that way" or "It sounds like that really bothered you."

4. **Manage Your Stress**: Use self-regulation techniques to stay calm during conflicts. When you feel yourself getting upset, take a few deep breaths, count to ten, or take a short break to cool down. This helps you approach the situation more calmly and rationally.

5. **Set Relationship Goals**: Work together to set goals for your relationship, such as spending more quality time together or improving communication. Sit down with your partner and discuss your relationship goals. Write them down and create a plan to achieve them. Regularly check in on your progress and celebrate your successes together.

6. **Practice Forgiveness**: Let go of grudges and focus on moving forward. When conflicts arise, focus on resolving

the issue rather than assigning blame. After a disagreement, discuss what you can learn from the experience and how you can prevent similar issues in the future. Practice letting go of resentment and forgiving your partner.

7. **Mindfulness Practice**: Practice mindfulness together to stay present and connected. Dedicate time each day to practice mindfulness activities, such as meditation, deep breathing exercises, or mindful walks. This can help you both stay grounded and connected.

8. **Regular Check-Ins**: Schedule regular check-ins to discuss your relationship and any issues that may have arisen. Use this time to express your feelings, listen to each other, and discuss ways to improve your relationship.

The Impact of Emotional Intelligence on Romantic Relationships

Applying emotional intelligence in your romantic relationship can significantly impact various aspects of your partnership, from emotional connection to conflict resolution. Here are some examples of how EI integration can influence your romantic relationship:

- **Emotional Connection**: By understanding and managing your emotions and those of your partner, you can build a deeper emotional connection and bond.

- **Conflict Resolution**: EI helps you approach conflicts with empathy and understanding, leading to healthier and more constructive resolutions.

- **Communication**: Effective use of EI enhances communication, reducing misunderstandings and fostering open and honest dialogue.

- **Relationship Satisfaction**: Couples with high EI tend to have more satisfying and fulfilling relationships, as they can navigate challenges and support each other effectively.

Personal Example: Jake and Emma, who had been together for three years, used EI to strengthen their relationship. They practiced active listening, expressed their emotions clearly, and showed empathy towards each other. By integrating these skills, they built a stronger emotional connection and improved their overall relationship satisfaction.

Building Sustainable Emotional Intelligence in Romantic Relationships

Building sustainable emotional intelligence in your romantic relationship is an ongoing process that requires regular practice and a genuine interest in personal growth. Here are some additional tips to help you maintain and enhance your EI integration over the long term:

1. **Stay Committed**: Regularly practice the techniques and

exercises discussed in this chapter. Consistency is key to developing and maintaining strong EI integration.

2. **Reflect and Adjust**: Regularly reflect on your progress and adjust your strategies as needed. Stay open to learning and growth.

3. **Seek Support**: Surround yourself with supportive people who encourage and motivate you to integrate EI into your relationship.

4. **Celebrate Successes**: Take time to celebrate your successes and milestones. Recognizing your achievements can boost your motivation and reinforce positive behavior.

5. **Stay Curious**: Cultivate a genuine interest in understanding yourself and your partner. Stay curious about your emotions and the emotions of your partner.

Conclusion

Emotional intelligence is a powerful tool that can enhance your romantic relationship by helping you understand and connect with your partner on a deeper level. By applying self-awareness, self-regulation, motivation, empathy, and social skills, you can navigate challenges, improve communication, and build a more loving and supportive partnership. In the next chapter, we'll explore practical applications of emotional intelligence in different areas of life, including personal relationships, academics, and professional settings.

9

EMOTIONAL INTELLIGENCE IN FAMILY DYNAMICS

Introduction

In the previous chapter, we explored how Emotional Intelligence (EI) can enhance romantic relationships. Now, let's dive into the importance of EI in family dynamics. Family relationships are some of the most significant and enduring connections we have, and using EI can help you build stronger bonds, improve communication, and navigate conflicts more effectively. In this chapter, we'll discuss the importance of EI in family relationships, how to build stronger bonds with family members, and how to navigate family conflicts with emotional intelligence.

Understanding the Importance of EI in Family Relationships

Family relationships are foundational to our emotional well-being. These connections can provide love, support, and a sense of belonging. However, they can also be sources of tension and conflict. Emotional Intelligence in family dynamics involves using self-awareness, self-regulation, motivation, empathy, and social skills to understand and connect with family members on a deeper level. It's about recognizing and managing your emotions and those of your family members to create a harmonious and supportive family environment.

Imagine you're having a disagreement with a sibling about household chores. Using EI, you can recognize your frustration (self-awareness), stay calm and avoid yelling (self-regulation), remember your commitment to a peaceful home (motivation), understand your sibling's perspective (empathy), and communicate effectively to find a compromise (social skills).

Benefits of Emotional Intelligence in Family Relationships

Applying EI in your family relationships offers numerous benefits, including:

- **Stronger Bonds**: EI helps you build deeper, more meaningful connections with family members.

- **Better Communication**: Effective use of EI enhances communication, reducing misunderstandings and conflicts.

- **Improved Conflict Resolution**: EI allows you to approach conflicts calmly and constructively, leading to healthier resolutions.

- **Increased Family Harmony**: Families with high EI tend to have more supportive and harmonious relationships.

Personal Example: Consider Alex and his family. When tensions rose during family gatherings, Alex used his EI skills to recognize his own stress (self-awareness), stay calm (self-regulation), focus on creating a positive atmosphere (motivation), understand his family members' perspectives (empathy), and communicate effectively to ease the tension (social skills). This approach helped create more harmonious family gatherings.

Techniques to Apply EI in Family Relationships

Developing and applying EI in your family relationships requires practice and intentional effort. Here are some techniques to help you get started:

1. **Practice Active Listening**: Truly listen to your family members without interrupting or planning your response.

   - **Detailed Practice**: When a family member is speaking, give them your full attention. Maintain eye contact, nod, and provide verbal affirmations like "I understand" or "That must be difficult." Reflect back what they've said to show you understand, such as "So, you're feeling upset because..."

2. **Express Your Emotions Clearly**: Use "I" statements to express your feelings without blaming your family members.

   - **Detailed Practice**: Instead of saying "You never listen to me," say "I feel unheard when I try to share my thoughts with you." This approach helps you take ownership of your emotions and reduces defensiveness.

3. **Show Empathy**: Understand and validate your family members' feelings, even if you don't agree with them.

   - **Detailed Practice**: If a family member is upset about something, try to understand their perspective. Say things like, "I can see why you're feeling that way" or "It sounds like that really bothered you."

4. **Manage Your Stress**: Use self-regulation techniques to stay calm during family conflicts.

   - **Detailed Practice**: When you feel yourself getting upset, take a few deep breaths, count to ten, or take a short break to cool down. This helps you approach the situation more calmly and rationally.

5. **Set Family Goals**: Work together to set goals for your family, such as spending more quality time together or improving communication.

○ **Detailed Practice**: Sit down with your family and discuss your family goals. Write them down and create a plan to achieve them. Regularly check in on your progress and celebrate your successes together.

6. **Practice Forgiveness**: Let go of grudges and focus on moving forward.

○ **Detailed Practice**: When conflicts arise, focus on resolving the issue rather than assigning blame. After a disagreement, discuss what you can learn from the experience and how you can prevent similar issues in the future. Practice letting go of resentment and forgiving your family members.

Personal Stories and Examples

Personal stories can make the concept of applying EI in family relationships more relatable. Let's look at some examples:

Alex's Journey: Improving Family Gatherings

Alex often found family gatherings stressful due to conflicting personalities and opinions. By applying EI, he was able to improve these gatherings significantly. Here's a detailed look at the steps he took:

1. **Recognizing His Emotions**: Alex identified that he often felt stressed and anxious before family gatherings (self-awareness).

2. **Staying Calm**: He practiced deep breathing exercises to stay calm during these gatherings (self-regulation).

3. **Focusing on Positivity**: Alex reminded himself of his goal to create a positive family atmosphere (motivation).

4. **Understanding Others**: He made a conscious effort to understand his family members' perspectives and feelings (empathy).

5. **Effective Communication**: Alex practiced active listening and used "I" statements to express his feelings without blaming others (social skills).

These steps helped Alex create a more harmonious atmosphere during family gatherings, making them more enjoyable for everyone.

Maria's Experience: Strengthening Bonds with Siblings

Maria felt distant from her siblings due to misunderstandings and lack of communication. By applying EI, she was able to strengthen her bonds with them. Here's a detailed look at the steps she took:

1. **Identifying the Problem**: Maria realized that she and her siblings often misunderstood each other and didn't communicate effectively (self-awareness).

2. **Practicing Active Listening**: She decided to practice active listening to improve their communication. When her siblings shared their feelings, Maria gave them her

full attention and reflected back what they said to show understanding.

3. **Expressing Emotions Clearly**: Maria used "I" statements to express her feelings without blaming her siblings. For example, she said, "I feel hurt when we don't spend time together," instead of "You never make time for me."

4. **Showing Empathy**: Maria made an effort to understand her siblings' perspectives and validate their feelings. She said things like, "I can see why you're feeling upset" or "It sounds like that really bothered you."

5. **Setting Family Goals**: They worked together to set goals for their relationship, such as having regular family dinners and improving communication.

6. **Practicing Forgiveness**: They made a commitment to let go of past grudges and focus on moving forward. After conflicts, they discussed what they could learn from the experience and how to avoid similar issues in the future.

These efforts helped Maria strengthen her bonds with her siblings and improve their overall relationship.

The Science Behind Emotional Intelligence in Family Relationships

Applying emotional intelligence in family relationships isn't just a feel-good concept; it has a strong scientific foundation. Research shows that families with high EI tend to have better communication, stronger emotional bonds, and greater family harmony.

Studies and Data:

- **Emotional Intelligence and Family Functioning**: A study published in the *Journal of Family Psychology* found that families with high EI have better overall family functioning. This is because they can manage their emotions, empathize with each other, and communicate effectively (Schutte, N.S., Malouff, J.M., & Bobik, C., 2001).

- **Emotional Intelligence and Conflict Resolution**: Research from the *Journal of Social and Personal Relationships* indicates that families with high EI are better at resolving conflicts. They approach disagreements with empathy and understanding, leading to healthier and more constructive resolutions (Brackett, M.A., Rivers, S.E., & Salovey, P., 2011).

- **Emotional Intelligence and Emotional Connection**: A study published in *Emotion* found that emotional intelligence enhances emotional connection among family members. Families who understand and manage their emotions are better able to connect on a deeper level (Zeidner, M., Matthews, G., & Roberts, R.D., 2012).

Practical Exercises

Here are some practical exercises to help you apply emotional intelligence in your family relationships:

1. **Active Listening**: Truly listen to your family members without interrupting or planning your response. Give them your full attention, maintain eye contact, nod, and provide verbal affirmations like "I understand" or "That must be difficult." Reflect back what they've said to show you understand, such as "So, you're feeling upset because…"

2. **Express Your Emotions Clearly**: Use "I" statements to express your feelings without blaming your family members. Instead of saying "You never listen to me," say "I feel unheard when I try to share my thoughts with you." This approach helps you take ownership of your emotions and reduces defensiveness.

3. **Show Empathy**: Understand and validate your family members' feelings, even if you don't agree with them. If a family member is upset about something, try to understand their perspective. Say things like, "I can see why you're feeling that way" or "It sounds like that really bothered you."

4. **Manage Your Stress**: Use self-regulation techniques to stay calm during family conflicts. When you feel yourself

getting upset, take a few deep breaths, count to ten, or take a short break to cool down. This helps you approach the situation more calmly and rationally.

5. **Set Family Goals**: Work together to set goals for your family, such as spending more quality time together or improving communication. Sit down with your family and discuss your family goals. Write them down and create a plan to achieve them. Regularly check in on your progress and celebrate your successes together.

6. **Practice Forgiveness**: Let go of grudges and focus on moving forward. When conflicts arise, focus on resolving the issue rather than assigning blame. After a disagreement, discuss what you can learn from the experience and how you can prevent similar issues in the future. Practice letting go of resentment and forgiving your family members.

7. **Mindfulness Practice**: Practice mindfulness together to stay present and connected. Dedicate time each day to practice mindfulness activities, such as meditation, deep breathing exercises, or mindful walks. This can help you both stay grounded and connected.

8. **Regular Family Meetings**: Schedule regular family meetings to discuss any issues, check in on each other's well-being, and set goals. Use this time to express your

feelings, listen to each other, and discuss ways to improve your family dynamics.

The Impact of Emotional Intelligence on Family Relationships

Applying emotional intelligence in your family relationships can significantly impact various aspects of your family dynamics, from emotional connection to conflict resolution. Here are some examples of how EI integration can influence your family relationships:

- **Emotional Connection**: By understanding and managing your emotions and those of your family members, you can build a deeper emotional connection and bond.

- **Conflict Resolution**: EI helps you approach conflicts with empathy and understanding, leading to healthier and more constructive resolutions.

- **Communication**: Effective use of EI enhances communication, reducing misunderstandings and fostering open and honest dialogue.

- **Family Harmony**: Families with high EI tend to have more supportive and harmonious relationships, as they can navigate challenges and support each other effectively.

Personal Example: Jake's family often had disagreements about household responsibilities, leading to tension and conflict.

By applying EI, Jake improved communication and conflict resolution within his family. He practiced active listening, expressed his emotions clearly, and showed empathy towards his family members. By setting family goals and practicing forgiveness, Jake helped create a more harmonious and supportive family environment.

Building Sustainable Emotional Intelligence in Family Relationships

Building sustainable emotional intelligence in your family relationships is an ongoing process that requires regular practice and a genuine interest in personal growth. Here are some additional tips to help you maintain and enhance your EI integration over the long term:

1. **Stay Committed**: Regularly practice the techniques and exercises discussed in this chapter. Consistency is key to developing and maintaining strong EI integration.

2. **Reflect and Adjust**: Regularly reflect on your progress and adjust your strategies as needed. Stay open to learning and growth.

3. **Seek Support**: Surround yourself with supportive people who encourage and motivate you to integrate EI into your family relationships.

4. **Celebrate Successes**: Take time to celebrate your successes and milestones. Recognizing your achievements

can boost your motivation and reinforce positive behavior.

5. **Stay Curious**: Cultivate a genuine interest in understanding yourself and your family members. Stay curious about your emotions and the emotions of your family members.

Conclusion

Emotional intelligence is a powerful tool that can enhance your family relationships by helping you understand and connect with your family members on a deeper level. By applying self-awareness, self-regulation, motivation, empathy, and social skills, you can navigate challenges, improve communication, and build a more supportive and harmonious family environment. In the next chapter, we'll explore practical applications of emotional intelligence in different areas of life, including personal relationships, academics, and professional settings.

10

Emotional Intelligence in Friendships

Introduction

We've talked about how Emotional Intelligence (EI) can improve your relationships with romantic partners and family members. Now, let's focus on another crucial area: friendships. Friendships are an essential part of our lives, providing support, companionship, and joy. Using EI can help you form and maintain these valuable connections, deepen your understanding and empathy, and manage conflicts and misunderstandings more effectively. In this chapter, we'll explore how EI can help in forming and maintaining friendships, deepening connections through empathy and understanding, and managing conflicts and misunderstandings.

Understanding the Importance of EI in Friendships

Friendships play a significant role in our emotional well-being. They provide a sense of belonging, reduce stress, and offer emotional support. Emotional Intelligence in friendships involves using self-awareness, self-regulation, motivation, empathy, and social skills to understand and connect with your friends on a deeper level. It's about recognizing and managing your emotions and those of your friends to create strong and lasting bonds.

Imagine you're having a disagreement with a friend about how to spend your weekend. Using EI, you can recognize your disappointment (self-awareness), stay calm and avoid arguing (self-regulation), remember your commitment to a supportive friendship (motivation), understand your friend's perspective (empathy), and communicate effectively to find a compromise (social skills).

Benefits of Emotional Intelligence in Friendships

Applying EI in your friendships offers numerous benefits, including:

- **Stronger Bonds**: EI helps you build deeper, more meaningful connections with your friends.

- **Better Communication**: Effective use of EI enhances communication, reducing misunderstandings and conflicts.

- **Improved Conflict Resolution**: EI allows you to approach conflicts calmly and constructively, leading to healthier resolutions.

- **Increased Friendship Satisfaction**: Friends with high EI tend to have more satisfying and fulfilling relationships.

Personal Example: Consider Emma and her friend Jake. When they faced disagreements, they used their EI skills to recognize their own emotions, stay calm, understand each other's perspectives, and communicate effectively. This approach helped them navigate challenges and build a stronger, more supportive friendship.

Techniques to Apply EI in Friendships

Developing and applying EI in your friendships requires practice and intentional effort. Here are some techniques to help you get started:

1. **Practice Active Listening**: Truly listen to your friends without interrupting or planning your response.

   - **Detailed Practice**: When a friend is speaking, give them your full attention. Maintain eye contact, nod, and provide verbal affirmations like "I understand" or "That must be difficult." Reflect back what they've said to show you understand, such as "So, you're feeling upset because…"

2. **Express Your Emotions Clearly**: Use "I" statements to express your feelings without blaming your friends.

   - **Detailed Practice**: Instead of saying "You never listen to me," say "I feel unheard when I try to share my thoughts with you." This approach helps you take ownership of your emotions and reduces defensiveness.

3. **Show Empathy**: Understand and validate your friends' feelings, even if you don't agree with them.

   ○ **Detailed Practice**: If a friend is upset about something, try to understand their perspective. Say things like, "I can see why you're feeling that way" or "It sounds like that really bothered you."

4. **Manage Your Stress**: Use self-regulation techniques to stay calm during conflicts.

   ○ **Detailed Practice**: When you feel yourself getting upset, take a few deep breaths, count to ten, or take a short break to cool down. This helps you approach the situation more calmly and rationally.

5. **Set Friendship Goals**: Work together to set goals for your friendship, such as spending more quality time together or improving communication.

   ○ **Detailed Practice**: Sit down with your friend and discuss your friendship goals. Write them down and create a plan to achieve them. Regularly check in on your progress and celebrate your successes together.

6. **Practice Forgiveness**: Let go of grudges and focus on moving forward.

   ○ **Detailed Practice**: When conflicts arise, focus on resolving the issue rather than assigning blame. After a disagreement, discuss what you can learn from the experience and how you can prevent similar issues in the future. Practice letting go of resentment and forgiving your friends.

Personal Stories and Examples

Personal stories can make the concept of applying EI in friendships more relatable. Let's look at some examples:

Alex and Maria's Journey: Strengthening Their Friendship

Alex and Maria had been friends since high school, but they faced challenges due to misunderstandings and lack of communication. By applying EI, they were able to strengthen their friendship significantly. Here's a detailed look at the steps they took:

1. **Identifying the Problem**: Alex and Maria realized that they often misunderstood each other and didn't communicate effectively (self-awareness).

2. **Practicing Active Listening**: They decided to practice active listening to improve their communication. When Maria shared her feelings, Alex gave her his full attention

and reflected back what she said to show understanding.

3. **Expressing Emotions Clearly**: They used "I" statements to express their feelings without blaming each other. For example, Maria said, "I feel hurt when we don't spend time together," instead of "You never make time for me."

4. **Showing Empathy**: They made an effort to understand each other's perspectives and validate their feelings. Alex said things like, "I can see why you're feeling upset" or "It sounds like that really bothered you."

5. **Setting Friendship Goals**: They worked together to set goals for their friendship, such as having regular catch-up sessions and improving communication.

6. **Practicing Forgiveness**: They made a commitment to let go of past grudges and focus on moving forward. After conflicts, they discussed what they could learn from the experience and how to avoid similar issues in the future.

These efforts helped Alex and Maria strengthen their friendship and improve their overall relationship.

Emma and Jake's Experience: Deepening Their Connection

Emma and Jake had been friends for a few years, but they wanted to deepen their emotional connection. By applying EI, they were able to achieve this. Here's a detailed look at the steps they took:

1. **Setting Friendship Goals**: They sat down together and discussed what they wanted to achieve in their friendship. They decided to spend more quality time together and practice mindfulness to stay connected.

2. **Quality Time Together**: They scheduled regular catch-up sessions to spend quality time together. They took turns planning activities, such as going for walks, having coffee, or watching a movie.

3. **Practicing Mindfulness Together**: They incorporated mindfulness practices into their routine. Every morning, they spent ten minutes meditating together. This practice helped them stay present and connected throughout the day.

4. **Managing Stress During Conflicts**: They worked on managing their stress during conflicts by taking breaks and using self-regulation techniques. If a disagreement became heated, they agreed to take a short break, cool down, and then come back to discuss the issue calmly.

5. **Active Listening**: They made a conscious effort to practice active listening. During their catch-up sessions, they listened to each other without interrupting and reflected back what the other person said to show understanding.

6. **Expressing Emotions Clearly**: They used "I" statements to express their feelings without blaming each oth-

er. For example, Emma said, "I feel hurt when you cancel our plans last minute," instead of "You always cancel our plans."

7. **Showing Empathy**: They practiced empathy by validating each other's feelings. When Jake shared his stress about work, Emma responded with empathy, saying, "I understand that you're under a lot of pressure. Let's figure out how we can support each other better."

These efforts helped Emma and Jake deepen their emotional connection and improve their overall friendship satisfaction.

The Science Behind Emotional Intelligence in Friendships

Applying emotional intelligence in friendships isn't just a feel-good concept; it has a strong scientific foundation. Research shows that friends with high EI tend to have better communication, stronger emotional bonds, and greater friendship satisfaction.

Studies and Data:

- **Emotional Intelligence and Friendship Satisfaction**: A study published in the *Journal of Social and Personal Relationships* found that individuals with high EI have higher levels of friendship satisfaction. This is because they can manage their emotions, empathize with their friends, and communicate effectively (Brackett, M.A.

, Warner, R.M., & Bosco, J.S., 2005).

- **Emotional Intelligence and Conflict Resolution**: Research from the *Journal of Social and Personal Relationships* indicates that friends with high EI are better at resolving conflicts. They approach disagreements with empathy and understanding, leading to healthier and more constructive resolutions (Lopes, P.N., Salovey, P., & Straus, R., 2003).

- **Emotional Intelligence and Emotional Connection**: A study published in *Emotion* found that emotional intelligence enhances emotional connection among friends. Friends who understand and manage their emotions are better able to connect on a deeper level (Zeidner, M., Matthews, G., & Roberts, R.D., 2012).

Practical Exercises

Here are some practical exercises to help you apply emotional intelligence in your friendships:

1. **Active Listening**: Truly listen to your friends without interrupting or planning your response. Give them your full attention, maintain eye contact, nod, and provide verbal affirmations like "I understand" or "That must be difficult." Reflect back what they've said to show you understand, such as "So, you're feeling upset because..."

2. **Express Your Emotions Clearly**: Use "I" statements to express your feelings without blaming your friends. Instead of saying "You never listen to me," say "I feel unheard when I try to share my thoughts with you." This approach helps you take ownership of your emotions and reduces defensiveness.

3. **Show Empathy**: Understand and validate your friends' feelings, even if you don't agree with them. If a friend is upset about something, try to understand their perspective. Say things like, "I can see why you're feeling that way" or "It sounds like that really bothered you."

4. **Manage Your Stress**: Use self-regulation techniques to stay calm during conflicts. When you feel yourself getting upset, take a few deep breaths, count to ten, or take a short break to cool down. This helps you approach the situation more calmly and rationally.

5. **Set Friendship Goals**: Work together to set goals for your friendship, such as spending more quality time together or improving communication. Sit down with your friend and discuss your friendship goals. Write them down and create a plan to achieve them. Regularly check in on your progress and celebrate your successes together.

6. **Practice Forgiveness**: Let go of grudges and focus on moving forward. When conflicts arise, focus on resolving

the issue rather than assigning blame. After a disagreement, discuss what you can learn from the experience and how you can prevent similar issues in the future. Practice letting go of resentment and forgiving your friends.

7. **Mindfulness Practice**: Practice mindfulness together to stay present and connected. Dedicate time each day to practice mindfulness activities, such as meditation, deep breathing exercises, or mindful walks. This can help you both stay grounded and connected.

8. **Regular Check-Ins**: Schedule regular check-ins to discuss your friendship and any issues that may have arisen. Use this time to express your feelings, listen to each other, and discuss ways to improve your friendship.

The Impact of Emotional Intelligence on Friendships

Applying emotional intelligence in your friendships can significantly impact various aspects of your relationships, from emotional connection to conflict resolution. Here are some examples of how EI integration can influence your friendships:

- **Emotional Connection**: By understanding and managing your emotions and those of your friends, you can build a deeper emotional connection and bond.

- **Conflict Resolution**: EI helps you approach conflicts with empathy and understanding, leading to healthier and more constructive resolutions.

- **Communication**: Effective use of EI enhances communication, reducing misunderstandings and fostering open and honest dialogue.

- **Friendship Satisfaction**: Friends with high EI tend to have more satisfying and fulfilling relationships, as they can navigate challenges and support each other effectively.

Personal Example: Jake and Emma, who had been friends for a few years, used EI to strengthen their friendship. They practiced active listening, expressed their emotions clearly, and showed empathy towards each other. By integrating these skills, they built a stronger emotional connection and improved their overall friendship satisfaction.

Building Sustainable Emotional Intelligence in Friendships

Building sustainable emotional intelligence in your friendships is an ongoing process that requires regular practice and a genuine interest in personal growth. Here are some additional tips to help you maintain and enhance your EI integration over the long term:

1. **Stay Committed**: Regularly practice the techniques and exercises discussed in this chapter. Consistency is key to developing and maintaining strong EI integration.

2. **Reflect and Adjust**: Regularly reflect on your progress and adjust your strategies as needed. Stay open to learning and growth.

3. **Seek Support**: Surround yourself with supportive people who encourage and motivate you to integrate EI into your friendships.

4. **Celebrate Successes**: Take time to celebrate your successes and milestones. Recognizing your achievements can boost your motivation and reinforce positive behavior.

5. **Stay Curious**: Cultivate a genuine interest in understanding yourself and your friends. Stay curious about your emotions and the emotions of your friends.

Conclusion

Emotional intelligence is a powerful tool that can enhance your friendships by helping you understand and connect with your friends on a deeper level. By applying self-awareness, self-regulation, motivation, empathy, and social skills, you can navigate challenges, improve communication, and build more supportive and fulfilling friendships. In the next chapter, we'll explore practical applications of emotional intelligence in different areas of life, including personal relationships, academics, and professional settings.

11

EMOTIONAL INTELLIGENCE IN THE WORKPLACE

Introduction

We've covered how Emotional Intelligence (EI) can enhance your romantic relationships, family dynamics, and friendships. Now, let's dive into the role of EI in the workplace. Professional relationships are crucial for career success and job satisfaction. Using EI in the workplace can help you build strong professional relationships, enhance teamwork and collaboration, and improve your leadership skills. In this chapter, we'll explore the role of EI in professional relationships, how to enhance teamwork and collaboration through EI, and the importance of EI in leadership.

Understanding the Role of EI in Professional Relationships

Professional relationships are essential for creating a positive and productive work environment. Emotional Intelligence in the workplace involves using self-awareness, self-regulation, motivation, empathy, and social skills to understand and connect with colleagues, managers, and clients. It's about recognizing and managing your emotions and those of others to foster a collaborative and supportive work environment.

Imagine you're working on a team project with tight deadlines. Using EI, you can recognize your stress (self-awareness), stay calm and focused (self-regulation), stay motivated to meet the deadlines (motivation), understand your team members' perspectives (empathy), and communicate effectively to coordinate efforts (social skills).

Benefits of Emotional Intelligence in the Workplace

Applying EI in your professional relationships offers numerous benefits, including:

- **Stronger Professional Relationships**: EI helps you build deeper, more meaningful connections with colleagues, managers, and clients.

- **Better Communication**: Effective use of EI enhances communication, reducing misunderstandings and conflicts.

- **Improved Teamwork and Collaboration**: EI allows you to work well in teams, fostering collaboration and mutual support.

- **Increased Job Satisfaction**: Employees with high EI tend to have higher job satisfaction and overall well-being.

Personal Example: Consider Emma, who used her EI skills to build strong professional relationships at her new job. When faced with challenging tasks, she used self-awareness to recognize her stress, self-regulation to stay calm, empathy to understand her colleagues' perspectives, and social skills to communicate effectively. This approach helped her create a positive work environment and succeed in her role.

Techniques to Apply EI in Professional Relationships

Developing and applying EI in your professional relationships requires practice and intentional effort. Here are some techniques to help you get started:

1. **Practice Active Listening**: Truly listen to your colleagues without interrupting or planning your response.

   - **Detailed Practice**: When a colleague is speaking, give them your full attention. Maintain eye contact, nod, and provide verbal affirmations like "I understand" or "That must be challenging." Reflect back what they've said to show you understand, such as "So, you're concerned about meeting the deadline because..."

2. **Express Your Emotions Clearly**: Use "I" statements to

express your feelings without blaming your colleagues.

- ○ **Detailed Practice**: Instead of saying "You never listen to my ideas," say "I feel unheard when I share my ideas and they're not acknowledged." This approach helps you take ownership of your emotions and reduces defensiveness.

3. **Show Empathy**: Understand and validate your colleagues' feelings, even if you don't agree with them.

   - ○ **Detailed Practice**: If a colleague is upset about a project, try to understand their perspective. Say things like, "I can see why you're feeling stressed about this" or "It sounds like you're really concerned about the outcome."

4. **Manage Your Stress**: Use self-regulation techniques to stay calm during high-pressure situations.

   - ○ **Detailed Practice**: When you feel yourself getting stressed, take a few deep breaths, count to ten, or take a short break to cool down. This helps you approach the situation more calmly and rationally.

5. **Set Professional Goals**: Work with your team to set goals for your projects, such as improving communication or increasing productivity.

○ **Detailed Practice**: Sit down with your team and discuss your project goals. Write them down and create a plan to achieve them. Regularly check in on your progress and celebrate your successes together.

6. **Practice Conflict Resolution**: Address conflicts with a calm and constructive attitude, seeking mutually beneficial solutions.

○ **Detailed Practice**: When a conflict arises, take a deep breath and approach the situation calmly. Listen to the other person's perspective and express your own feelings without blame. Work together to find a solution that satisfies both parties.

Personal Stories and Examples

Personal stories can make the concept of applying EI in professional relationships more relatable. Let's look at some examples:

Alex and Maria's Journey: Enhancing Teamwork

Alex and Maria worked on a team project at their company but often faced challenges due to miscommunication and conflicting ideas. By applying EI, they were able to enhance their teamwork significantly. Here's a detailed look at the steps they took:

1. **Identifying the Problem**: Alex and Maria realized that their team often miscommunicated and didn't collaborate effectively (self-awareness).

2. **Practicing Active Listening**: They decided to practice active listening to improve their communication. When Maria shared her ideas, Alex gave her his full attention and reflected back what she said to show understanding.

3. **Expressing Emotions Clearly**: They used "I" statements to express their feelings without blaming each other. For example, Alex said, "I feel frustrated when our meetings go off track," instead of "You always derail our meetings."

4. **Showing Empathy**: They made an effort to understand each other's perspectives and validate their feelings. Maria said things like, "I can see why you're feeling overwhelmed" or "It sounds like you're really concerned about the deadline."

5. **Setting Professional Goals**: They worked together with their team to set goals for their project, such as improving communication and increasing productivity.

6. **Practicing Conflict Resolution**: They addressed conflicts with a calm and constructive attitude, seeking mutually beneficial solutions. After conflicts, they discussed what they could learn from the experience and how to avoid similar issues in the future.

These efforts helped Alex and Maria enhance their teamwork and improve their overall project outcomes.

Emma's Experience: Leading with EI

Emma, a team leader at her company, wanted to improve her leadership skills by applying EI. Here's a detailed look at the steps she took:

1. **Self-Awareness**: Emma regularly reflected on her emotions and how they affected her leadership. She identified that she often felt stressed and overwhelmed during busy periods.

2. **Self-Regulation**: She practiced self-regulation techniques to stay calm and composed. When she felt stressed, she took deep breaths, counted to ten, and took short breaks to cool down.

3. **Motivation**: Emma stayed motivated by setting clear goals for herself and her team. She reminded herself of the importance of her role and the positive impact she could have on her team.

4. **Empathy**: She made a conscious effort to understand her team members' perspectives and validate their feelings. When a team member was struggling, Emma said things like, "I understand that this project is challenging. Let's figure out how we can support you better."

5. **Social Skills**: Emma practiced active listening, clear communication, and conflict resolution. She regularly checked in with her team, listened to their concerns, and

worked with them to find solutions.

These efforts helped Emma become a more effective leader and create a positive and supportive work environment.

The Science Behind Emotional Intelligence in the Workplace

Applying emotional intelligence in the workplace isn't just a feel-good concept; it has a strong scientific foundation. Research shows that employees with high EI tend to have better communication, stronger teamwork, and greater job satisfaction.

Studies and Data:

- **Emotional Intelligence and Job Performance**: A study published in the *Journal of Organizational Behavior* found that individuals with high EI tend to have better job performance. This is because they can manage their emotions, empathize with colleagues, and communicate effectively (O'Boyle, E.H., Humphrey, R.H., Pollack, J. M., Hawver, T.H., & Story, P.A., 2011).

- **Emotional Intelligence and Leadership**: Research from the *Harvard Business Review* indicates that leaders with high EI are more effective. They are better at managing teams, making decisions, and driving organizational success (Goleman, D., 1998).

- **Emotional Intelligence and Teamwork**: A study published in *Group & Organization Management* found that teams with high EI have better teamwork and collaboration. This is because they can manage conflicts, understand each other's perspectives, and communicate effectively (Jordan, P.J., Ashkanasy, N.M., & Hartel, C.E.J., 2002).

Practical Exercises

Here are some practical exercises to help you apply emotional intelligence in your professional relationships:

1. **Active Listening**: Truly listen to your colleagues without interrupting or planning your response. Give them your full attention, maintain eye contact, nod, and provide verbal affirmations like "I understand" or "That must be challenging." Reflect back what they've said to show you understand, such as "So, you're concerned about meeting the deadline because..."

2. **Express Your Emotions Clearly**: Use "I" statements to express your feelings without blaming your colleagues. Instead of saying "You never listen to my ideas," say "I feel unheard when I share my ideas and they're not acknowledged." This approach helps you take ownership of your emotions and reduces defensiveness.

3. **Show Empathy**: Understand and validate your col-

leagues' feelings, even if you don't agree with them. If a colleague is upset about a project, try to understand their perspective. Say things like, "I can see why you're feeling stressed about this" or "It sounds like you're really concerned about the outcome."

4. **Manage Your Stress**: Use self-regulation techniques to stay calm during high-pressure situations. When you feel yourself getting stressed, take a few deep breaths, count to ten, or take a short break to cool down. This helps you approach the situation more calmly and rationally.

5. **Set Professional Goals**: Work with your team to set goals for your projects, such as improving communication or increasing productivity. Sit down with your team and discuss your project goals. Write them down and create a plan to achieve them. Regularly check in on your progress and celebrate your successes together.

6. **Practice Conflict Resolution**: Address conflicts with a calm and constructive attitude, seeking mutually beneficial solutions. When a conflict arises, take a deep breath and approach the situation calmly. Listen to the other person's perspective and express your own feelings without blame. Work together to find a solution that satisfies both parties.

7. **Mindfulness Practice**: Practice mindfulness to stay pre-

sent and focused. Dedicate time each day to practice mindfulness activities, such as meditation, deep breathing exercises, or mindful walks. This can help you stay grounded and manage stress more effectively.

8. **Regular Check-Ins**: Schedule regular check-ins with your team to discuss any issues, check in on each other's well-being, and set goals. Use this time to express your feelings, listen to each other, and discuss ways to improve your teamwork and collaboration.

The Impact of Emotional Intelligence on Professional Relationships

Applying emotional intelligence in your professional relationships can significantly impact various aspects of your work environment, from emotional connection to conflict resolution. Here are some examples of how EI integration can influence your professional relationships:

- **Emotional Connection**: By understanding and managing your emotions and those of your colleagues, you can build a deeper emotional connection and bond.

- **Conflict Resolution**: EI helps you approach conflicts with empathy and understanding, leading to healthier and more constructive resolutions.

- **Communication**: Effective use of EI enhances communication, reducing misunderstandings and fostering open and honest dialogue.

- **Job Satisfaction**: Employees with high EI tend to have higher job satisfaction and overall well-being, as they can navigate challenges and support each other effectively.

Personal Example: Jake, a project manager, used EI to improve his team's collaboration. He practiced active listening, expressed his emotions clearly, and showed empathy towards his team members. By integrating these skills, he built a stronger emotional connection with his team and improved their overall job satisfaction and productivity.

Building Sustainable Emotional Intelligence in the Workplace

Building sustainable emotional intelligence in your professional relationships is an ongoing process that requires regular practice and a genuine interest in personal growth. Here are some additional tips to help you maintain and enhance your EI integration over the long term:

1. **Stay Committed**: Regularly practice the techniques and exercises discussed in this chapter. Consistency is key to developing and maintaining strong EI integration.

2. **Reflect and Adjust**: Regularly reflect on your progress

and adjust your strategies as needed. Stay open to learning and growth.

3. **Seek Support**: Surround yourself with supportive people who encourage and motivate you to integrate EI into your professional relationships.

4. **Celebrate Successes**: Take time to celebrate your successes and milestones. Recognizing your achievements can boost your motivation and reinforce positive behavior.

5. **Stay Curious**: Cultivate a genuine interest in understanding yourself and your colleagues. Stay curious about your emotions and the emotions of your colleagues.

Conclusion

Emotional intelligence is a powerful tool that can enhance your professional relationships by helping you understand and connect with your colleagues, managers, and clients on a deeper level. By applying self-awareness, self-regulation, motivation, empathy, and social skills, you can navigate challenges, improve communication, and build a more supportive and productive work environment. In the next chapter, we'll explore practical applications of emotional intelligence in different areas of life, including personal relationships, academics, and professional settings.

12

Practical Exercises and Activities

Introduction

Throughout the previous chapters, we've explored how Emotional Intelligence (EI) can enhance your relationships with romantic partners, family members, friends, and colleagues. Now, let's dive into practical exercises and activities that can help you enhance your EI on a daily basis. These exercises are designed to improve your self-awareness, self-regulation, empathy, and social skills. We'll also include journaling prompts and reflection activities to deepen your understanding and application of EI. Let's get started!

Daily Practices to Enhance Emotional Intelligence

Developing EI is an ongoing process that requires regular practice. Here are some daily practices to help you enhance your EI:

1. **Mindfulness Meditation**: Practicing mindfulness meditation can help you stay present and aware of your emo-

tions.

- ○ **Detailed Practice**: Set aside 10-15 minutes each day for mindfulness meditation. Sit comfortably, close your eyes, and focus on your breath. When your mind wanders, gently bring your attention back to your breath. This practice can help you stay calm, recognize your emotions, and respond thoughtfully to various situations.

2. **Gratitude Journaling**: Keeping a gratitude journal can help you focus on positive emotions and experiences.

- ○ **Detailed Practice**: Each day, write down three things you are grateful for. These can be big or small things, such as a supportive friend, a delicious meal, or a beautiful sunset. Reflecting on what you're grateful for can enhance your overall emotional well-being.

3. **Emotional Check-Ins**: Regularly checking in with yourself can help you stay aware of your emotions and how they're affecting you.

- ○ **Detailed Practice**: Set aside a few moments each day to check in with yourself. Ask yourself, "How am I feeling right now?" and "What might be causing these feelings?" This practice can help you stay connected to your emotions and understand their impact on your behavior.

4. **Acts of Kindness**: Performing acts of kindness can boost your empathy and strengthen your social connections.

- **Detailed Practice**: Each day, perform a small act of kindness for someone else. This could be as simple as giving a compliment, helping a colleague with a task, or sending a supportive message to a friend. These acts of kindness can enhance your empathy and build stronger relationships.

Exercises for Improving Self-Awareness, Self-Regulation, Empathy, and Social Skills

Here are some specific exercises to help you improve various components of EI:

1. Self-Awareness Exercise: Body Scan Meditation

- **Detailed Practice**: Set aside 10-15 minutes for a body scan meditation. Lie down in a comfortable position and close your eyes. Slowly bring your attention to different parts of your body, starting from your toes and working your way up to your head. Notice any sensations, tension, or discomfort without judgment. This practice can help you become more aware of your physical and emotional state.

2. Self-Regulation Exercise: Pause and Reflect

- **Detailed Practice**: When you find yourself in a stressful situation, practice pausing and reflecting before reacting. Take a few deep breaths and ask yourself, "What am I feeling right now?" and "How do I want to respond?" This practice can help you manage your emotions and respond more calmly and effectively.

3. Empathy Exercise: Perspective-Taking

- **Detailed Practice**: Choose a situation where you had

a disagreement with someone. Reflect on the situation and try to see it from the other person's perspective. Ask yourself, "How might they have been feeling?" and "What might have been their motivations?" This exercise can help you develop a deeper understanding of others' emotions and perspectives.

4. Social Skills Exercise: Active Listening Practice

○ **Detailed Practice**: Practice active listening with a friend or family member. During a conversation, focus entirely on the other person. Avoid interrupting, and reflect back what they've said to show understanding. For example, "It sounds like you're feeling frustrated because..." This practice can enhance your communication skills and strengthen your relationships.

Journaling Prompts and Reflection Activities

Journaling can be a powerful tool for developing EI. Here are some journaling prompts and reflection activities to deepen your understanding and application of EI:

1. Self-Awareness Journaling Prompt

- **Prompt**: Reflect on a recent situation where you felt a strong emotion. Describe the situation, the emotion you felt, and any physical sensations you experienced. What thoughts went through your mind? How did you respond to the emotion? What did you learn about yourself from this experience?

2. Self-Regulation Journaling Prompt

- **Prompt**: Think of a time when you successfully managed a difficult emotion. Describe the situation and the emotion you felt. What strategies did you use to regulate your emotion? How did these strategies affect the outcome of the situation? What can you learn from this experience to apply in future situations?

3. Empathy Journaling Prompt

- **Prompt**: Reflect on a recent interaction with someone where you felt empathy for them. Describe the situation and the other person's emotions. How did you respond to their feelings? How did your response affect the interaction? What can you learn from this experience to enhance your empathy in future interactions?

4. **Social Skills Journaling Prompt**

   ○ **Prompt**: Think of a recent conversation where you felt you communicated effectively. Describe the conversation and the strategies you used to communicate. How did the other person respond? What worked well, and what could you improve? What can you learn from this experience to enhance your communication skills?

5. **Reflection Activity: Emotional Intelligence Assessment**

   ○ **Activity**: Take an emotional intelligence assessment to evaluate your current EI skills. There are many online assessments available, such as the Emotional Intelligence Appraisal by Travis Bradberry and Jean Greaves. Reflect on your results and identify areas where you excel and areas where you can improve. Set specific goals for enhancing your EI skills and create a plan to achieve them.

6. **Reflection Activity: Goal Setting for EI**

- ○ **Activity**: Set specific, measurable, achievable, relevant, and time-bound (SMART) goals for developing your EI. For example, "I will practice mindfulness meditation for 10 minutes each day for the next month" or "I will use 'I' statements to express my emotions in conversations with my partner." Regularly review your goals and track your progress.

The Science Behind Practical Exercises for EI

The benefits of these practical exercises are supported by scientific research. Here are some studies that highlight the effectiveness of these practices:

- **Mindfulness Meditation and Emotional Regulation**: Research published in the *Journal of Consulting and Clinical Psychology* found that mindfulness meditation can enhance emotional regulation and reduce symptoms of anxiety and depression (Hofmann, S.G., Sawyer, A.T., Witt, A.A., & Oh, D., 2010).

- **Gratitude Journaling and Well-Being**: A study published in the *Journal of Personality and Social Psychology* found that gratitude journaling can increase overall well-being and life satisfaction (Emmons, R.A., & McCullough, M.E., 2003).

- **Active Listening and Communication**: Research from the *International Journal of Listening* indicates that active listening can improve communication and strengthen relationships (Bodie, G.D., 2011).

The Impact of Practical Exercises on Emotional Intelligence

Incorporating these practical exercises into your daily routine can significantly impact various aspects of your emotional intelligence. Here are some examples of how these exercises can influence your EI:

- **Self-Awareness**: Regular journaling and mindfulness meditation can help you become more aware of your emotions and how they affect your behavior.

- **Self-Regulation**: Practicing mindfulness and reflection can improve your ability to manage your emotions and respond calmly in stressful situations.

- **Empathy**: Engaging in perspective-taking exercises and acts of kindness can enhance your ability to understand and empathize with others.

- **Social Skills**: Practicing active listening and effective communication can improve your social interactions and strengthen your relationships.

Building Sustainable Emotional Intelligence

Building sustainable emotional intelligence is an ongoing process that requires regular practice and a genuine interest in personal growth. Here are some additional tips to help you maintain and enhance your EI over the long term:

1. **Stay Committed**: Regularly practice the techniques and exercises discussed in this chapter. Consistency is key to

developing and maintaining strong EI.

2. **Reflect and Adjust**: Regularly reflect on your progress and adjust your strategies as needed. Stay open to learning and growth.

3. **Seek Support**: Surround yourself with supportive people who encourage and motivate you to enhance your EI.

4. **Celebrate Successes**: Take time to celebrate your successes and milestones. Recognizing your achievements can boost your motivation and reinforce positive behavior.

5. **Stay Curious**: Cultivate a genuine interest in understanding yourself and others. Stay curious about your emotions and the emotions of those around you.

Conclusion

Enhancing your emotional intelligence is a powerful way to improve your relationships, well-being, and overall success. By incorporating practical exercises and activities into your daily routine, you can develop self-awareness, self-regulation, empathy, and social skills. In the next chapter, we'll explore practical applications of emotional intelligence in different areas of life, including personal relationships, academics, and professional settings.

Conclusion

We've come a long way on this journey of exploring and developing Emotional Intelligence (EI). Throughout the chapters, we've delved into the core components of EI—self-awareness, self-regulation, motivation, empathy, and social skills—and applied these principles to various aspects of life, including romantic relationships, family dynamics, friendships, and the workplace. In this final chapter, we'll recap the key concepts, encourage you to continue developing your EI, and leave you with some final thoughts and inspiration for your journey ahead.

Recap of Key Concepts

1. **Self-Awareness**:

   - **Understanding Emotions**: Recognizing and understanding your emotions is the first step in developing EI. It involves being aware of how your emotions influence your thoughts and behaviors.

- **Practical Exercise**: We discussed mindfulness meditation and body scan meditation as tools to enhance self-awareness. These practices help you become more attuned to your emotional states and physical sensations.

2. **Self-Regulation**:

- **Managing Emotions**: Self-regulation is about managing your emotions, especially in stressful situations. It involves staying calm, thinking before reacting, and maintaining control over your emotional responses.

- **Practical Exercise**: Techniques like deep breathing, counting to ten, and taking breaks were highlighted to help manage emotions effectively.

3. **Motivation**:

- **Intrinsic Motivation**: This involves doing things because they are personally rewarding, rather than for external rewards. Intrinsic motivation drives you to pursue your goals and overcome challenges.

- **Practical Exercise**: Setting clear, achievable goals and creating vision boards were discussed as ways to boost motivation and stay focused on your objectives.

4. **Empathy**:

○ **Understanding Others**: Empathy is the ability to understand and share the feelings of others. It involves putting yourself in someone else's shoes and responding with compassion.

○ **Practical Exercise**: Perspective-taking and acts of kindness were emphasized as methods to enhance empathy and build stronger connections.

5. **Social Skills**:

○ **Effective Communication**: Social skills are about interacting harmoniously with others. They include active listening, clear communication, conflict resolution, and teamwork.

○ **Practical Exercise**: Practicing active listening, using "I" statements, and engaging in role-playing scenarios were suggested to improve social skills.

Encouragement to Continue Developing EI

Developing EI is not a one-time effort but an ongoing journey. Here are some reasons why continuing to work on your EI is important:

1. **Personal Growth**:

○ **Lifelong Learning**: EI contributes to your overall

personal growth. As you continue to develop your EI, you'll find yourself becoming more self-aware, resilient, and adaptable. This lifelong learning process enriches your life and opens up new opportunities for growth and success.

2. Improved Relationships:

- **Stronger Bonds**: High EI enhances your ability to build and maintain healthy relationships. Whether it's with family, friends, colleagues, or romantic partners, EI helps you connect on a deeper level and navigate conflicts more effectively.

3. Career Success:

- **Professional Advantage**: In the workplace, EI is a key differentiator. Employees and leaders with high EI are better at teamwork, communication, and leadership, which leads to greater career success and job satisfaction.

4. Mental Health:

- **Emotional Well-Being**: Developing EI can significantly improve your mental health. It helps you manage stress, cope with challenges, and maintain a positive outlook on life. Studies have shown that individuals with high EI experience lower levels of anxiety and depression (Mayer, J.D., & Salovey, P., 1997).

Final Thoughts and Inspiration for Your Journey

1. **Embrace the Journey**:

   - **Continuous Improvement**: Remember that developing EI is a continuous journey. Embrace the process, celebrate your progress, and be patient with yourself. Every step you take towards improving your EI is a step towards a more fulfilling and successful life.

2. **Stay Curious**:

   - **Lifelong Learning**: Cultivate a curious mindset. Stay open to learning new things about yourself and others. Seek out new experiences, ask questions, and remain curious about the world around you.

3. **Build a Support System**:

   - **Community Support**: Surround yourself with supportive people who encourage and motivate you. Share your journey with friends, family, or a mentor. A strong support system can provide valuable feedback and keep you accountable.

4. **Practice Self-Compassion**:

○ **Be Kind to Yourself**: Developing EI can be challenging, and it's important to practice self-compassion. Be kind to yourself, acknowledge your efforts, and forgive yourself for any setbacks. Remember that growth takes time and effort.

5. Inspire Others:

○ **Lead by Example**: As you develop your EI, you can inspire others to do the same. Lead by example and share your experiences and insights with those around you. By promoting EI, you can contribute to a more compassionate and understanding world.

Practical Data and Studies to Support Your Journey

1. Emotional Intelligence and Job Performance:

○ **Study**: A meta-analysis published in the *Journal of Organizational Behavior* found that individuals with high EI tend to have better job performance. This is because they can manage their emotions, empathize with colleagues, and communicate effectively (O'Boyle, E.H., Humphrey, R.H., Pollack, J.M., Hawver, T.H., & Story, P.A., 2011).

2. Emotional Intelligence and Mental Health:

- **Study**: Research published in the *Journal of Personality and Social Psychology* found that individuals with high EI experience lower levels of anxiety and depression. This is because they can better manage their emotions and cope with stress (Mayer, J.D., & Salovey, P., 1997).

3. **Emotional Intelligence and Relationship Satisfaction**:

- **Study**: A study published in the *Journal of Social and Personal Relationships* found that couples with high EI have higher levels of relationship satisfaction. This is because they can manage their emotions, empathize with their partners, and communicate effectively (Brackett, M.A., Warner, R.M., & Bosco, J.S., 2005).

Final Encouragement

As you continue your journey of developing EI, remember that every step you take is valuable. Embrace the process, stay curious, and practice self-compassion. Celebrate your progress and be patient with yourself. By committing to this journey, you are investing in a more fulfilling, successful, and emotionally intelligent future.

Inspiration Quote: "Emotional intelligence is the key to both personal and professional success. By understanding and managing our emotions, we can navigate life's challenges with grace and build deeper, more meaningful connections with those around us." – Daniel Goleman

Conclusion

Developing Emotional Intelligence is a lifelong journey that can transform your life. By focusing on self-awareness, self-regulation, motivation, empathy, and social skills, you can improve your relationships, enhance your well-being, and achieve greater success in both personal and professional settings. Embrace the journey, stay committed, and inspire others along the way. Your dedication to developing EI will lead to a more fulfilling and emotionally intelligent life.

13

ABOUT THE AUTHOR

Alexandra Hart is a renowned psychiatrist with a deep passion for personal growth and emotional well-being. With over a decade of experience in the field, Alexandra has helped countless individuals understand and manage their emotions through the power of Emotional Intelligence. Her work as a psychiatrist has provided her with invaluable insights into the human mind, which she shares in her writing and coaching.

Alexandra's empathetic approach and practical strategies have empowered people to improve their relationships, excel in their careers, and achieve greater overall happiness. She combines her professional expertise with a genuine care for others, making her a trusted guide on the journey to emotional mastery.

When she's not writing or practicing psychiatry, Alexandra enjoys painting, volunteering at local shelters, and spending time with her family and friends. Her commitment to personal development and emotional health shines through in her work, inspiring others to live more fulfilling lives.